TRIK 1.0

Contract Bridge
for the Apple II

Jim Hilger

Produced by:
Brian Wiser & Bill Martens

 Apple PugetSound Program Library Exchange

Trik 1.0: Contract Bridge for the Apple II

www.callapple.org

ISBN: 978-1-387-80020-9

ACKNOWLEDGEMENTS

Trik is a program that Jim Hilger wrote and released in 1980 as part of A.P.P.L.E.'s *DiskPak 7* disks along with a number of games. He also provided all of the original art for the program manual.

PRODUCTION

Brian Wiser → Design, Layout, Editing, Cover
Bill Martens → Typesetting, Proofreading
Jim Hilger → Original Art

DISCLAIMER

About Jim Hilger

Jim Hilger was an Apple II programmer who was involved in the early years of the Apple Pugetsound Program Library Exchange (A.P.P.L.E.) user group. He is the creator of some of the famous artwork which appeared over the years in the magazine as well as the original logo for *Call-A.P.P.L.E.* magazine.

Jim contributed a number of items both to the A.P.P.L.E. Public Domain Library as well as to the periodic *DISKPAK* libraries which *TRIK 1.0* is part of. He was also the author of all of the additional programs included on the *DISKPAK 7A* and *7B* floppy disks released in 1983.

About the Producers

Brian Wiser

Brian Wiser is a producer of books, films, games, and events, as well as a long-time consultant, enthusiast and historian of Apple, the Apple II and Macintosh. Steve Wozniak and Steve Jobs, as well as *Creative Computing*, *Nibble*, *InCider*, and *A+* magazines were early influences.

Brian designed, edited, and co-produced dozens of books including: *Nibble Viewpoints: Business Insights From The Computing Revolution*, *Cyber Jack: The Adventures of Robert Clardy and Synergistic Software*, *Synergistic Software: The Early Games*, *The Colossal Computer Cartoon Book: Enhanced Edition*, *All About Applesoft: Enhanced Edition*, *Graphically Speaking: Enhanced Edition*, *What's Where in the Apple: Enhanced Edition*, and *The WOZPAK: Special Edition* – an important Apple II historical book with Steve Wozniak's restored original, technical handwritten notes. Brian is also the author of *The Etch-a-Sketch and Other Fun Programs*.

He passionately preserves and archives all facets of Apple's history, and noteworthy companies such as Beagle Bros and Applied Engineering, featured on AppleArchives.com. His writing, interviews and books are featured on the technology news site CallApple.org and in *Call-A.P.P.L.E.* magazine that he co-produces as an A.P.P.L.E. board member. Brian also co-produced the retro iOS game *Structris*.

In 2005, Brian was cast as an extra in Joss Whedon's movie *Serenity*, leading him to being a producer and director for the documentary film *Done The Impossible: The Fans' Tale of Firefly & Serenity*. He brought some of the *Firefly* cast aboard his Browncoat Cruise and recruited several of the *Firefly* cast to appear in a film for charity. Throughout these experiences, he develops close personal relationships with many actors, authors, and computer industry luminaries. Brian speaks about his adventures to large audiences at conventions around the country.

Bill Martens

Bill Martens is a systems engineer specializing in office infrastructures and has been programming since 1976. The DEC PDP 11/40 with ASR-33 Teletypes and CRT's were his first computing platforms with his first forays in the Apple world coming with the Apple II computer.

Influences in Bill's computing life came from *Byte* magazine, *Creative Computing* magazine, and *Call-A.P.P.L.E.* magazine as well as his mentors Samuel Perkins, Don Williams, Joff Morgan, and Mike Christensen.

Bill is the author of *ApPilot/W1*, *Beyond Quest*, *The Anatomy of an EAMON*, and multiple EAMon adventure games, as well as a co-producer of many books including *What's Where in the Apple: Enhanced Edition*, *The WOZPAK: Special Edition*, *Nibble Viewpoints: Business Insights From The Computing Revolution*, and co-programmer for the iOS version of the retro game *Structris*. He has written many articles which have appeared in user group newsletters and magazines such as Call-A.P.P.L.E..

Bill worked for Apple Pugetsound Program Library Exchange (A.P.P.L.E.) under Val Golding and Dick Hubert as a data manager and programmer in the 1980s, and is the current president of the A.P.P.L.E. user group established in 1978. He reorganized A.P.P.L.E. and restarted *Call-A.P.P.L.E.* magazine in 2002. He is the production editor for the A.P.P.L.E. website CallApple.org, writes science fiction novels in his spare time, and is a retired semi-pro football player.

CONTENTS

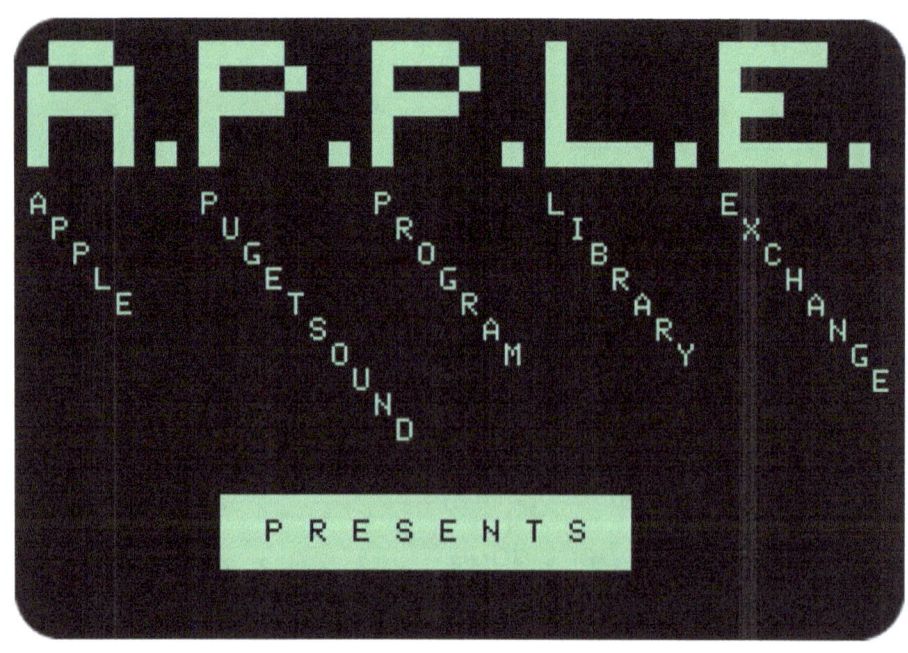

How to Begin

TRIK 1.0 was originally included in the A.P.P.L.E. Diskpak 7A and 7B which was released in 1983. It was written in Integer BASIC by Jim Hilger and made available with manual by A.P.P.L.E. staff members.

The first thing that you will need is the diskette containing the fly-by-night software:

- TRIK 1.0 BID
- TRIK 1.0 PLAY
- BUILD-A-HAND

The only other item that might be nice to have is an Apple II computer with at least 32K of memory and a Disk II floppy disk drive.

The diskette has been remade by A.P.P.L.E. and now boots straight to the *TRIK 1.0* game menu. The disk image is available from: www.callapple.org. You will need to insert the diskette into the drive and boot into DOS. If however you are using the original Trik 1.0 disks, they are DOS 3.2 and you will need to boot BASIC first.

Once you have booted the disk, a menu will appear on the screen offering you two choices. Select the first choice on the menu.

You will now be running the TRIK 1.0 BID program.

How to BID

A colorful title screen will soon appear on the display. In the text area of the screen, there will be a copyright message which will disappear within a short span of time and be replaced with the following message

DUPLICATE PLAY? (Y/N):

It is now time for you to begin making decisions about your hand. Type either a Y for Yes or an N for No and press the RETURN key. Once you have chosen, the computer will take one of the two following actions depending on your selection:

- If you press the N key – This tells TRIK 1.0 BID to shuffle the cards thoroughly (and randomly) and to deal out four hands. The computer will also randomly designate which hand has been dealt.

- If you press the Y Key – This tells TRIK 1.0 BID to select a hand which has been previously stored on the diskette, distribute the hands, and designate which hand has been dealt.

If you chose the Yes option, then the program will ask you which pre-stored set of hands you desire by printing the prompt:

SAVED HAND NUMBER?

You will need to tell the computer the number of the hand which you would like to try. This selection is a number between 1 and 10, corresponding to the pre-stored hands which we have provided on the disk. Each one of these pre-stored hands has its own interesting quirks and will not be an easy play.

3

Once you have made your choice of the options, there will be a pause while the computer shuffles and deals the hands. The computer will not ask you to cut the cards, however, I assure you that it is scrupulously honest!

The computer will now clear the screen and display your bridge hand. You will always play the SOUTH hand. After some brief time to think about it, your hand will be announced by the computer and the bidding will begin.

The Dealer will bid first. When it is your turn to bid, please consult a Bridge book before continuing. For convenience, I have supplied some short hand codes for you to use when it is your turn to bid.

The Codes

Code to Enter	*Meaning*
PA	Pass
DB	Double
RD	Re-Double
1H	1 of Hearts
2S	2 of Spades
3D	3 of Diamonds
4C	4 of Clubs
5N	5 with No Trump

Other Codes

Clearly we have left out a number of bids but, you should be able to deduce other possibilities from the examples in the code table. You can enter the code for your bid to play that bid or you can just press RETURN without entering a code to pass.

When the bidding has concluded, press RETURN and you will be presented with a menu containing five options. They are:

```
1. DISPLAY THE HANDS

2. PLAY OUT THE HANDS

3. REBID THE SAME HANDS

4. GET A NEW DEAL

5. END
```

To choose an option from the menu, press the number corresponding with the preferred option. You do not need to press RETURN.

If you choose option 2 (PLAY OUT THE HANDS) then you will want to refer to the next section of this manual (How to Play). All of the other choices on the menu should be self explanatory.

Note: The bidding conventions used are as follows: Take-Out Double, Short Clubs, Four Card Majors, and most Goren bidding conventions.

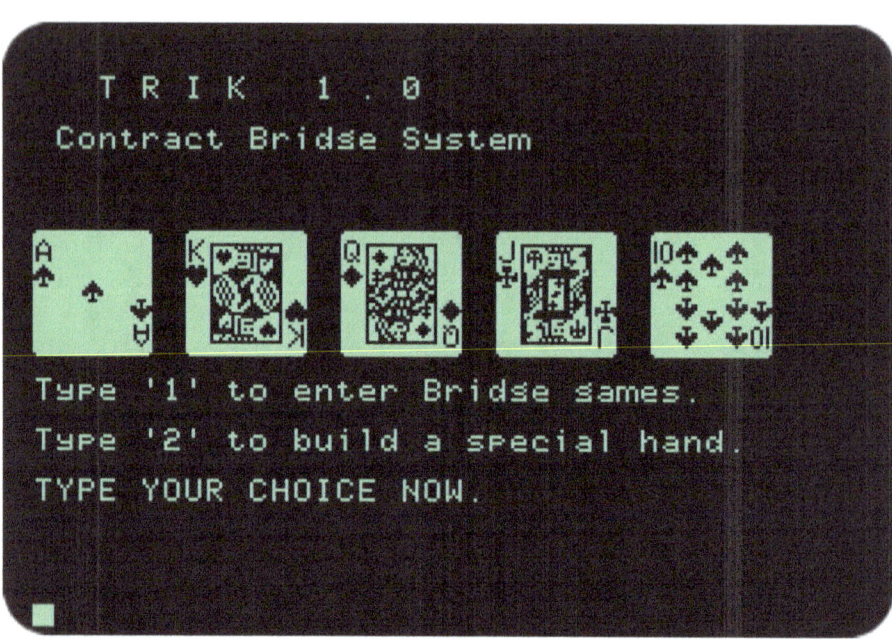

T R I K   1 . 0
Contract Bridge System

Type '1' to enter Bridge games.

Type '2' to build a special hand.

TYPE YOUR CHOICE NOW.

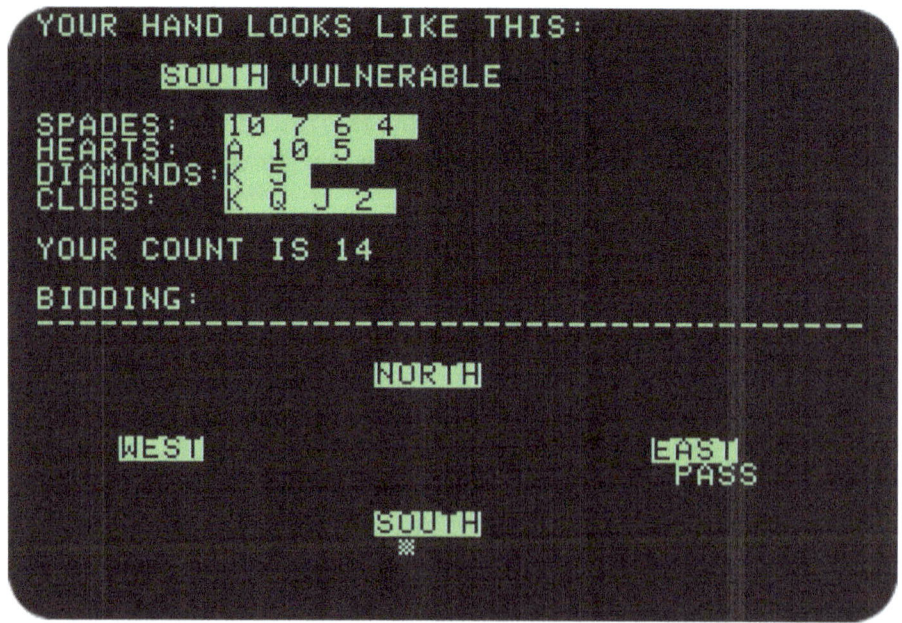

YOUR HAND LOOKS LIKE THIS:

SOUTH VULNERABLE

SPADES: 10 7 6 4
HEARTS: A 10 5
DIAMONDS: K 5
CLUBS: K Q J 2

YOUR COUNT IS 14

BIDDING:

                    NORTH

     WEST   EAST
                                 PASS

                    SOUTH
                      ※

How to Play

There will be a pause as TRIK 1.0 BID executes the CHAIN to TRIK1.0 PLAY. If EAST/WEST are the declarer, you will be asked to swap hands with EAST or WEST, since TRIK 1.0 PLAY only plays defense. If NORTH/SOUTH are the declarer then no hand switching is necessary.

Next NORTH becomes the dummy and WEST begins thinking about what to lead. Since WEST is thinking in Integer BASIC, it takes a number of seconds to actually play. During play, you will always play for the dummy (NORTH) and SOUTH, while the computer will always play for EAST and WEST. A flashing question mark will appear whenever it is your turn to play a card.

Once again, you are provided with a number of short-hand codes for entering the cards you wish to play. They are show in the Play Codes section.

As with the bidding, once you enter the code you wish to play, you need to press the Return key. If the code is not a valid code, the computer will buzz disgustingly at you, and await a proper play.

Play Codes

The following codes are a subset of the play codes which will allow you to play a particular hand.

Code to Play	Meaning
AH	Ace of Hearts
KC	King of Clubs
TD	Ten of Diamonds
5S	5 of spades

The Count

The current count of tricks won will be maintained at the bottom of the display screen. The "WE" denotes the NORTH / SOUTH.

If, at any time when you are to make a play, you believe that you can easily capture all of the remaining tricks, type LD (for Lay Down) and press the RETURN key twice. The computer will then automatically award you the remaining tricks.

After all of the tricks are taken, press RETURN and a new menu screen will display with the five choices shown:

```
1. DISPLAY THE HANDS

2. SAVE THIS HAND

3. REPLAY THIS CONTRACT

4. DEAL A NEW HAND

5. END
```

Outside of the second option on the menu (SAVE THIS HAND), the rest of the hands should be self explanatory. The second option is explained in the next section.

Saving Hands

There are two ways to save hands. The first way is by selection option two from the menu. You will be requested to assign a number between 1 and 99 to the hands played so that they may be stored on the diskette for re-use at a future date. While there are 99 possible hands, the reality is that the first 10 are already spoken for.

The first 10 hands on the disk are the demo hands which we have stored for your usages. Thus, that leaves 11 through 99 for a total of 89 possible hands. For the sake of clarity and ease of remembering what number you are using, we recommend starting with hand number 11 and going from there even though you are not required to save hands in sequential order.

The other method for saving Bridge hands involves the BUILD-A-HAND program. This program can be entered immediately after booting the diskette by selecting option 2 from the menu, or by entering RUN BUILD-A-HAND from the Integer BASIC or Applesoft Prompt.

BUILD-A-HAND allows you to specify exactly what cards you wish to have appear in each hand. You enter the cards using the same codes in in TRIK 1.0 PLAY (AH, KC, TD, 5S, Etc...) and pressing RETURN after entering each card code. This is good for trying out hands appearing in newspaper Bridge columns and other sources for Contract Bridge.

As with the first method of saving hands, you will be asked to assign a hand number to your creation.

And So...

That is about all you will need to know about using the *TRIK 1.0* program. We have included a guide to Contract Bridge from Wikipedia in the next section of the book in order to give the user a bit more background on the game itself.

It is our sincere hope that you will enjoy the programs and that they will help you improve your game.

TRIK 1.0 is not a static entity and improvements are planned. If you have suggestions on how to improve the program, feel free to send them to www.callapple.org via our contact page.

Items which are not talked about in the manual are:

- In the first version of *TRIK*, WEST always lead first in PLAY even if NORTH was really the declarer. This has been corrected in the version included on this disk.

- *TRIK 1.0* is was a bit shy about bidding slams. The version provided here is a bit more educated in slam bidding.

- TRIK EAST, WEST, and NORTH would not double a bid (with the exception of take out doubles) when they think the bid can be set. This capability has been added.

What is Contract Bridge?

Contract bridge, or simply **bridge**, is a trick-taking card game using a standard 52-card deck. Trick Taking is a card or tile-based game in which play of a *hand* centers on a series of finite rounds or units of play, called *tricks*, which are each evaluated to determine a winner or *taker* of that trick. The object of such games then may be closely tied to the number of tricks taken, as in **plain-trick games** such as contract bridge, whist, and spades, or to the value of the cards contained in taken tricks, as in **point-trick games** such as Pinochle, the Tarot family, Briscola, and most evasion games like Hearts. **Trick-and-draw games** are trick-taking games in which the players can fill up their hands after each trick. In most variants, players are free to play any card into a trick in the first phase of the game, but must *follow suit* as soon as the stock is depleted. **Trick-avoidance games** like Reversis or Polignac are those in which the aim is to avoid taking some or all tricks.

In its basic format, Contract Bridge is played by four players in two competing partnerships, with partners sitting opposite each other around a table. Millions of people play bridge worldwide in clubs, tournaments, online and with friends at home, making it one of the world's most popular card games, particularly among seniors. The World Bridge Federation (WBF) is the governing body for international competitive bridge, with numerous other bodies governing bridge at the regional level.

The game consists of a number of deals, each progressing through four phases. The cards are dealt to the players, and then the players *call* (or *bid*) in an auction seeking to take the contract, specifying how many tricks the partnership receiving the contract (the declaring side) needs to take to receive points for the deal. During the auction, partners use their bids to also exchange information about their hands, including overall strength and distribution of the suits; no other means of conveying or implying any information is permitted. The cards are then played, the declaring side trying to fulfill the contract, and the defenders trying to stop the declaring side from achieving its goal. The deal is scored based on the number of tricks taken, the contract, and various other factors which depend to some extent on the variation of the game being played.

Rubber bridge is the most popular variation for casual play, but most club and tournament play involves some variant of duplicate bridge, in which the cards are not re-dealt on each occasion, but the same deal is played by two or more sets of players (or "tables") to enable comparative scoring.

History of the Game

Bridge is a member of the family of trick-taking games and is a derivative of whist, which had become the dominant such game and enjoyed a loyal following for centuries. The idea of a trick-taking 52-card game has its first documented origins in Italy and France. The French physician and author Rabelais (1493–1553) mentions a game called "La Triomphe" in one of his works. In 1526 the Italian Francesco Berni wrote the oldest known (as of 1960) textbook on a game very similar to whist, known as "Triomfi". Also, a Spanish textbook in Latin from the first half of the 16th century, "Triumphens Historicus", deals with the same subject.

Bridge departed from whist with the creation of "Biritch" in the 19th century and evolved through the late 19th and early 20th centuries to form the present game. The first rule book for bridge, dated 1886, is *Biritch, or Russian Whist* written by John Collinson, an English financier working in Ottoman Constantinople (now Istanbul). It and his subsequent letter to *The Saturday Review* dated 28 May 1906, document the origin of *Biritch* as being the Russian community in Constantinople. The word *biritch* is thought to be a transliteration of the Russian word Бирюч (бирчий, бирич), an occupation of a diplomatic clerk or an announcer. Another theory is that British soldiers invented the game bridge while serving in the Crimean War, and named it after the Galata Bridge, which they crossed on their way to a coffeehouse to play cards.

Biritch had many significant bridge-like developments: dealer chose the trump suit, or nominated his partner to do so; there was a call of no trumps (*biritch*); dealer's partner's hand became dummy; points were scored above and below the line; game was 3NT, 4♥ and 5♦ (although 8 club odd tricks and 15 spade odd tricks were needed); the score could be doubled and redoubled; and there were slam bonuses. It has some features in common with solo whist. This game, and variants of it known as "bridge" and "bridge whist", became popular in the United States and the United Kingdom in the 1890s despite the long-established dominance of whist. Its breakthrough was its acceptance in 1894 by Lord Brougham at London's Portland Club.

In 1904 auction bridge was developed, in which the players bid in a competitive auction to decide the contract and declarer. The object became to make at least as many tricks as were contracted for, and penalties were introduced for failing to do so. Auction bridge bidding beyond winning the auction is pointless. If taking all 13 tricks, there is no difference in score between a 1♠ and a 7♠ final bid, as no bonus for game, small slam or grand slam exists.

The modern game of contract bridge was the result of innovations to the scoring of auction bridge by Harold Stirling Vanderbilt and others. The most significant change was that only the tricks contracted for were scored below the line toward game or a slam bonus, a change that resulted in bidding becoming much more challenging and interesting. Also new was the concept of "vulnerability", making sacrifices to protect the lead in a rubber more expensive. The various scores were adjusted to produce a more balanced and interesting game. Vanderbilt set out his rules in 1925, and within a few years contract bridge had so supplanted other forms of the game that "bridge" became synonymous with "contract bridge".

The form of bridge mostly played in clubs, tournaments and online is duplicate bridge. The number of people playing contract bridge has declined since its peak in the 1940s, when a survey found it was played in 44% of US households. The game is still widely played, especially amongst retirees, and in 2005 the ACBL estimated there were 25 million players in the US.

How the Game is Played

Overview

Bridge is a four-player partnership trick-taking game with thirteen tricks per deal. The dominant variations of the game are rubber bridge, more common in social play; and duplicate bridge, which enables comparative scoring in tournament play. Each player is dealt thirteen cards from a standard 52-card deck. A trick starts when a player leads, i.e. plays the first card. The leader to the first trick is determined by the auction; the leader to each subsequent trick is the player who won the preceding trick. Each player, in clockwise order, plays one card on the trick. Players must play a card of the same suit as the original card led, unless they have none (said to be "void"), in which case they may play any card.

The player who played the highest-ranked card wins the trick. Within a suit, the ace is ranked highest followed by the king, queen and jack and then the ten through to the two. In a deal where the auction has determined that there is no trump suit, the trick must be won by a card of the suit led. However, in a deal where there is a trump suit, cards of that suit are superior in rank to any of the cards of any other suit. If one or more players plays a trump to a trick when void in the suit led, the highest trump wins. For example, if the trump suit is spades and a player is void in the suit led and plays a spade card, they win the trick if no other player plays a higher spade. If a trump suit is led, the usual rule for trick-taking applies.

Unlike its predecessor, whist, the goal of bridge is not simply to take the most tricks in a deal. Instead, the goal is to successfully estimate how many tricks one's partnership can take. To illustrate this, the simpler partnership trick-taking game of spades has a similar mechanism: the usual trick-taking rules apply with the trump suit being spades, but in the beginning of the game, players *bid* or estimate how many tricks they can win, and the number of tricks bid by both players in a partnership are added. If a partnership takes at least that many tricks, they receive points for the round; otherwise, they receive penalty points.

Bridge extends the concept of bidding into an auction, where partnerships compete to take a contract, specifying how many tricks they will need to take in order to receive points, and also specifying the trump suit (or no trump, meaning that there will be no trump suit). Players take turns to call in a clockwise order: each player in turn either passes, doubles – which increases the penalties for not making the contract specified by the opposing partnership's last bid, but also increases the reward for making it – or redoubles, or states a contract that their partnership will adopt, which must be higher than the previous highest bid (if any). Eventually, the player who bid the highest contract – which is determined by the contract's level as well as the trump suit or no trump – wins the contract for their partnership.

In the example auction below, the east–west pair secures the contract of 6♠; the auction concludes when there have been three successive passes. Note that six tricks are added to contract values, so the six-level contract would actually be a contract of twelve tricks. In practice, establishing a contract without enough information on the other partner's hand is difficult, so there exist many bidding systems assigning meanings to bids, with common ones including Standard American, Acol, and 2/1 game forcing. Contrast with Spades, where players only have to bid their own hand.

After the contract is decided, and the first lead is made, the declarer's partner (dummy) lays their cards face up on the table, and the declarer plays the dummy's cards as well as their own. The opposing partnership is called the defenders, and their goal is to stop the declarer from fulfilling his contract. Once all the cards have been played, the hand is scored: if the declaring side make their contract, they receive points based on the level of the contract, with some trump suits being worth more points than others and no trump being the highest, as well as bonus points for overtricks. But if the declarer fails to fulfil the contract, the defenders receive points depending on the declaring side's undertricks (the number of tricks short of the contract) and whether the contract was doubled by the defenders.

Setup and Dealing

The four players sit in two partnerships with players sitting opposite their partners. A cardinal direction is assigned to each seat, so that one partnership sits in North and South, while the other sits in West and East. The cards may be freshly dealt or, in duplicate bridge games, pre-dealt. All that is needed in basic games are the cards and a method of keeping score, but there is often other equipment on the table, such as a board containing the cards to be played (in duplicate bridge), bidding boxes, or screens.

In rubber bridge, each player draws a card at the start of the game with the player who drew the highest cards dealing first. The second highest card becomes the dealer's partner and takes the chair on the opposite side of the table. They play against the other two. The deck is shuffled and cut, usually by the player to the left of the dealer, before dealing. Players take turns to deal, in clockwise order. The dealer deals the cards clockwise, one card at a time. Normally rubber bridge is played with two packs of cards and whilst one pack is being dealt, the dealer's partner shuffles the other pack. After shuffling the pack is placed on the right ready for the next dealer. ("If you're not an idiot quite. Put the cards on the right.") Before dealing, the next dealer passes the cards to the previous dealer who cuts them.

In duplicate bridge, the cards are pre-dealt, either by hand or by a computerized dealing machine, in order to allow for competitive scoring. Once dealt, the cards are placed in a device called a "board", having slots designated for each player's cardinal direction seating position. After a deal has been played, players return their cards to the appropriate slot in the board, ready to be played by the next table.

Auction

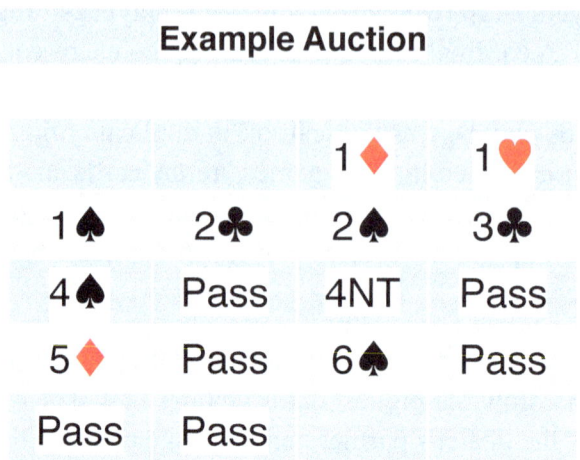

Example Auction

		1♦	1♥
1♠	2♣	2♠	3♣
4♠	Pass	4NT	Pass
5♦	Pass	6♠	Pass
Pass	Pass		

East-West and north–south compete for the contract. East-West prevail, specifying the trump suit (spades) and the minimum number of tricks beyond six which they must win, six.

The dealer opens the auction and can make the first call, and the auction proceeds clockwise. When it is their turn to call, a player may pass – but can enter into the bidding later – or bid a contract, specifying the level of their contract and either the trump suit or no trump (the denomination), provided that it is higher than the last bid by any player, including their partner. All bids promise to take a number of tricks in excess of six, so a bid must be between one (seven tricks) and seven (thirteen tricks). A bid is higher than another bid if either the level is greater (e.g., 2♣ over 1NT) or the denomination is higher, with the order being in ascending order: ♣, ♦, ♥, ♠, and NT (no trump). Calls may be made orally or with a bidding box (digitally in online bridge).

If the last bid was by the opposing partnership, one may also double the opponents' bid, increasing the penalties for undertricks, but also increasing the reward for making the contract. Doubling does not carry to future bids by the opponents unless future bids are doubled again. A player on the opposing partnership being doubled may also redouble, which increases the penalties and rewards further. Players may not see their partner's hand during the auction, only their own. There exist many bidding conventions that assign agreed meanings to various calls to assist players in reaching an optimal contract (or obstruct the opponents).

The auction ends when, after a player bids, doubles, or redoubles, every other player has passed, in which case the action proceeds to the play; or every player has passed and no bid has been made, in which case the round is considered to be "passed out" and not played.

Play

The player from the declaring side who first bid the denomination named in the final contract becomes declarer. The player left to the declarer leads to the first trick. Dummy then lays his or her cards face-up on the table, organized in columns by suit. Play proceeds clockwise, with each player required to follow suit if possible. Tricks are won by the highest trump, or if there were none played, the highest card of the led suit. The player who won the previous trick leads to the next trick. The declarer has control of the dummy's cards and tells his partner which card to play at dummy's turn. There also exist conventions that communicate further information between defenders about their hands during the play.

At any time, a player may claim, stating that their side will win a specific number of the remaining tricks. The claiming player lays his cards down on the table and explains the order in which he intends to play the remaining cards. The opponents can either accept the claim and the round is scored accordingly, or dispute the claim. If the claim is disputed, play continues with the claiming player's cards face up in rubber games, or in duplicate games, play ceases and the tournament director is called to adjudicate the hand.

Scoring

At the end of the hand, points are awarded to the declaring side if they make the contract, or else to the defenders. Partnerships can be vulnerable, increasing the rewards for making the contract, but also increasing the penalties for undertricks. In rubber bridge, if a side has won 100 contract points, they have won a game and are vulnerable for the remaining rounds, but in duplicate bridge, vulnerability is predetermined based on the number of each board.

If the declaring side makes their contract, they receive points for odd tricks, or tricks bid and made in excess of six. In both rubber and duplicate bridge, the declaring side is awarded 20 points per odd trick for a contract in clubs or diamonds, and 30 points per odd trick for a contract in hearts or spades. For a contract in notrump, the declaring side is awarded 40 points for the first odd trick and 30 points for the remaining odd tricks. Contract points are doubled or quadrupled if the contract is respectively doubled or redoubled.

In rubber bridge, a partnership wins one game once it has accumulated 100 contract points; excess contract points do not carry over to the next game. A partnership that wins two games wins the rubber, receiving a bonus of 500 points if the opponents have won a game, and 700 points if they have not.

Overtricks score the same number of points per odd trick, although their doubled and redoubled values differ. Bonuses vary between the two bridge variations both in score and in type (for example, rubber bridge awards a bonus for holding a certain combination of high cards), although some are common between the two.

A larger bonus is awarded if the declaring side makes a small slam or grand slam, a contract of 12 or 13 tricks respectively. If the declaring side is not vulnerable, a small slam gets 500 points, and a grand slam 1000 points. If the declaring side is vulnerable, a small slam is 750 points and a grand slam is 1,500.

In rubber bridge, the rubber finishes when a partnership has won two games, but the partnership receiving the most *overall* points wins the rubber. Duplicate bridge is scored comparatively, meaning that the score for the hand is compared to other tables playing the same cards and match points are scored according to the comparative results: usually either "matchpoint scoring", where each partnership receives 2 points (or 1 point) for each pair that they beat, and 1 point (or ½ point) for each tie; or IMPs (international matchpoint) scoring, where the number of IMPs varies (but less than proportionately) with the points difference between the teams.

Undertricks are scored in both variations as follows:

Points per Undertrick

Undertricks	Vulnerable			Not Vulnerable		
	Undoubled	Doubled	Redoubled	Undoubled	Doubled	Redoubled
1st undertrick		200	400		100	200
2nd and 3rd, each	100	300	600	50	200	400
4th and each subsequent		300	600		300	600

Rules

The rules of the game are referred to as the *laws* as promulgated by various bridge organizations.

Laws of Duplicate Bridge

The official rules of duplicate bridge are promulgated by the WBF as "The Laws of Duplicate Bridge 2017". The Laws Committee of the WBF, composed of world experts, updates the Laws every 10 years; it also issues a Laws Commentary advising on interpretations it has rendered.

In addition to the basic rules of play, there are many additional rules covering playing conditions and the rectification of irregularities, which are primarily for use by tournament directors who act as referees and have overall control of procedures during competitions. But various details of procedure are left to the discretion of the zonal bridge organization for tournaments under their aegis and some (for example, the choice of movement) to the sponsoring organization (for example, the club).

Some zonal organizations of the WBF also publish editions of the Laws. For example, the American Contract Bridge League (ACBL) publishes the Laws of Duplicate Bridge and additional documentation for club and tournament directors.

Rules of Rubber Bridge

There are no universally accepted rules for rubber bridge, but some zonal organizations have published their own. An example for those wishing to abide by a published standard is *The Laws of Rubber Bridge* as published by the American Contract Bridge League.

The majority of rules mirror those of duplicate bridge in the bidding and play and differ primarily in procedures for dealing and scoring.

Game Strategy

Bidding

Much of the complexity in bridge arises from the difficulty of arriving at a good final contract in the auction (or deciding to let the opponents declare the contract). This is a difficult problem: the two players in a partnership must try to communicate enough information about their hands to arrive at a makeable contract, but the information they can exchange is restricted – information may be passed only by the calls made and later by the cards played, not by other means; in addition, the agreed-upon meaning of each call and play must be available to the opponents.

Since a partnership that has freedom to bid gradually at leisure can exchange more information, and since a partnership that can interfere with the opponents' bidding (as by raising the bidding level rapidly) can cause difficulties for their opponents, bidding systems are both informational and strategic. It is this mixture of information exchange and evaluation, deduction, and tactics that is at the heart of bidding in bridge.

A number of basic rules of thumb in bridge bidding and play are summarized as bridge maxims.

Bidding Systems and Conventions

A *bidding system* is a set of partnership agreements on the meanings of bids. A partnership's bidding system is usually made up of a core system, modified and complemented by specific conventions (optional customizations incorporated into the main system for handling specific bidding situations) which are pre-chosen between the partners prior to play. The line between a well-known convention and a part of a system is not always clear-cut: some bidding systems include specified conventions by default. Bidding systems can be divided into mainly natural systems such as Acol and Standard American, and mainly artificial systems such as the Precision Club and Polish Club.

Calls are usually considered to be either *natural* or *conventional* (artificial). A natural call carries a meaning that reflects the call; a natural bid intuitively showing hand or suit strength based on the level or suit of the bid, and a natural double expressing that the player believes that the opposing partnership will not make their contract. By contrast, a conventional (artificial) call offers and/or asks for information by means of pre-agreed coded interpretations, in which some calls convey very specific information or requests that are not part of the natural meaning of the call. Thus in response to 4NT, a 'natural' bid of 5♦ would state a preference towards a diamond suit or a desire to play the contract in 5 diamonds, whereas if the partners have agreed to use the common Blackwood convention, a bid of 5♦ in the same situation would say nothing about the diamond suit, but tell the partner that the hand in question contains exactly one ace.

Conventions are valuable in bridge because of the need to pass information beyond a simple like or dislike of a particular suit, and because the limited bidding space can be used more efficiently by adopting a conventional (artificial) meaning for a given call where a natural meaning would have less utility, because the information it would convey is not valuable or because the desire to convey that information would arise only rarely. The conventional meaning conveys more useful (or more frequently useful) information. There are a very large number of conventions from which players can choose; many books have been written detailing bidding conventions. Well-known conventions include Stayman (to ask the opening 1NT bidder to show any four-card major suit), Jacoby transfers (a request by (usually) the weak hand for the partner to bid a particular suit first, and therefore to become the declarer), and the Blackwood convention (to ask for information on the number of aces and kings held, used in slam bidding situations).

The term *preempt* refers to a high-level tactical bid by a weak hand, relying upon a very long suit rather than high cards for tricks. Preemptive bids serve a double purpose – they allow players to indicate they are bidding on the basis of a long suit in an otherwise weak hand, which is important information to share, and they also consume substantial bidding space which prevents a possibly strong opposing pair from exchanging information on their cards. Several systems include the use of opening bids or other early bids with weak hands including long (usually six to eight card) suits at the 2, 3 or even 4 or 5 levels as preempts.

Basic Natural Systems

As a rule, a natural suit bid indicates a holding of at least four (or more, depending on the situation and the system) cards in that suit as an opening bid, or a lesser number when supporting partner; a natural NT bid indicates a balanced hand.

Most systems use a count of high card points as the basic evaluation of the strength of a hand, refining this by reference to shape and distribution if appropriate. In the most commonly used point count system, aces are counted as 4 points, kings as 3, queens as 2, and jacks as 1 point; therefore, the deck contains 40 points. In addition, the *distribution* of the cards in a hand into suits may also contribute to the strength of a hand and be counted as distribution points. A better than average hand, containing 12 or 13 points, is usually considered sufficient to *open* the bidding, i.e., to make the first bid in the auction. A combination of two such hands (i.e., 25 or 26 points shared between partners) is often sufficient for a partnership to bid, and generally to make, game in a major suit or notrump (more are usually needed for a minor suit game, as the level is higher).

In natural systems, a 1NT opening bid usually reflects a hand that has a relatively balanced shape (usually between two and four (or less often five) cards in each suit) and a sharply limited number of high card points, usually somewhere between 12 and 18 – the most common ranges use a span of exactly three points (for example, 12–14, 15–17 or 16–18), but some systems use a four-point range, usually 15–18.

Opening bids of three or higher are preemptive bids, i.e., bids made with weak hands that especially favor a particular suit, opened at a high level in order to define the hand's value quickly and to frustrate the opposition. For example, a hand of ♠ KQJ9872 ♥ 7 ♦ 42 ♣ 763 would be a candidate for an opening bid of 3♠, designed to make it difficult for the opposing team to bid and find their optimum contract even if they have the bulk of the points, as it is nearly valueless unless spades are trumps, it contains good enough spades that the penalty for being set should not be higher than the value of an opponent game, and the high card weakness makes it more likely that the opponents have enough strength to make game themselves.

Openings at the 2 level are either unusually strong (2NT, natural, and 2♣, artificial) or preemptive, depending on the system. Unusually strong bids communicate an especially high number of points (normally 20 or more) or a high trick-taking potential (normally 8 or more). Also 2♦ as the strongest (by HCP and by DP+HCP) has become more common, perhaps especially at websites that offer duplicate bridge. Here the 2♣ opening is used for either hands with a good 6-card suit or longer (max one losing card) and a total of 18 HCP up to 23 total points – or "2

+ ½NT", like 2NT but with 22–23 HCP. Whilst the 2♦ opening bid takes care of all hands with 24 points (HCP or with distribution points included) with the only exception of "Gambling 3NT".

Opening bids at the one level are made with hands containing 12–13 points or more and which are not suitable for one of the preceding bids. Using Standard American with 5-card majors, opening hearts or spades usually promises a 5-card suit. Partnerships who agree to play 5-card majors open a minor suit with 4-card majors and then bid their major suit at the next opportunity. This means that an opening bid of 1♣ or 1♦ will sometimes be made with only 3 cards in that suit. Doubles are sometimes given conventional meanings in otherwise mostly natural systems. A natural, or *penalty* double, is one used to try to gain extra points when the defenders are confident of setting (defeating) the contract. The most common example of a conventional double is the takeout double of a low-level suit bid, implying support for the unbid suits or the unbid major suits and asking partner to choose one of them.

Variations on the Basic Themes

Bidding systems depart from these basic ideas in varying degrees. Standard American, for instance, is a collection of conventions designed to bolster the accuracy and power of these basic ideas, while Precision Club is a system that uses the 1♣ opening bid for all or almost all strong hands (but sets the threshold for "strong" rather lower than most other systems – usually 16 high card points) and may include other artificial calls to handle other situations (but it may contain natural calls as well). Many experts today use a system called 2/1 game forcing (enunciated as two over one game forcing), which amongst other features adds some complexity to the treatment of the one notrump response as used in Standard American. In the UK, Acol is the most common system; its main features are a weak one notrump opening with 12–14 high card points and several variations for 2-level openings.

There are also a variety of advanced techniques used for hand evaluation. The most basic is the Milton Work point count, (the 4-3-2-1 system detailed above) but this is sometimes modified in various ways, or either augmented or replaced by other approaches such as losing trick count, honor point count, law of total tricks, or Zar Points.

Common conventions and variations within natural systems include:

- *Blackwood* (either the original version or *Roman Key Card*)

- How the partnership's bidding practices will be varied if their opponents intervene or compete.

- Point count required for 1 NT opening bid ('mini' 10–12, 'weak' 12–14, 'strong' 15–17 or 16–18)

- *Stayman* (together with Blackwood, described as "the two most famous conventions in Bridge".)

- What types of *cue bids (e.g. bidding the opponents' suit)* the partnership will play, if any.

- Whether 1♣ (and sometimes 1♦) is 'natural' or 'suspect' *(also called 'phoney' or 'short')*, signifying an opening hand lacking a notable heart or spade suit

- Whether an opening bid of 1♥ and 1♠ requires a minimum of 4 or 5 cards in the suit (*4 or 5 card majors*)

- Whether doubling a contract at the 1, 2 and sometimes higher levels signifies a belief that the opponents' contract will fail and a desire to raise the stakes (a *penalty double*), or an indication of strength but no biddable suit coupled with a request that partner bid something (a *takeout double*).

- Whether doubling or overcalling over opponents' 1NT is natural or conventional. One common artificial agreement is Cappelletti, where 2♣ is a transfer to be passed or corrected to a major, 2♦ means both majors and a major shows that suit plus a minor.

- Whether opening bids at the two level are 'strong' (20+ points) or 'weak' (i.e., pre-emptive with a 6 card suit). (Note: an opening bid of 2♣ is usually played in otherwise natural systems as conventional, signifying any exceptionally strong hand)

- Whether the partnership will play *Jacoby transfers* (bids of 2♦ and 2♥ over 1NT or 3♦ and 3♥ over 2NT respectively require the 1NT or 2NT bidder to rebid 2♥ and 2♠ or 3♥ and 3♠), *minor suit transfers* (bids of 2♠ and either 2NT or 3♣ over 1NT respectively require the 1NT bidder to bid 3♣ and 3♦) and *Texas transfers* (bids of 4♦ and 4♥ respectively require the 1NT, or 2NT bidder to rebid 4♥ and 4♠)

- Which (if any) bids are *forcing* and require a response.

Within play, it is also commonly agreed what systems of opening leads, signals and discards will be played:

- Conventions for the opening lead govern how the first card to be played will be chosen and what it will mean,

- Count signals cover the situation when a defender is following suit (usually to a suit that the declarer has led). In such circumstances the order in which a defender plays his spot cards will indicate whether an even or odd number of cards was originally held in that suit. This can help the other defender count out the entire original distribution of the cards in that suit. It is sometimes critical to know this when defending.

- Discards cover the situation when a defender cannot follow suit and therefore has free choice what card to play or throw away. In such circumstances the thrown-away card can be used to indicate some aspect of the hand, or a desire for a specific suit to be played.

- Signals indicate how cards played within a suit are chosen – for example, playing a noticeably high card when this would not be expected can signal encouragement to continue playing the suit, and a low card can signal discouragement and a desire for partner to choose some other suit. (Some partnerships use "reverse" signals, meaning that a noticeably high card *discourages* that suit and a noticeably low card *encourages* that suit, thus not "wasting" a potentially useful intermediate card in the suit of interest.)

- Suit preference signals cover the situation where a defender is returning a suit which will be ruffed by his partner. If he plays a high card he is showing an entry in the higher side suit and vice versa. There are some other situations where this tool may be used.

- Surrogate signals cover the situation when it is critical to show length in a side suit and it will be too late if defenders wait until that suit is played. Then, the play in the first declarer played suit is a count signal regarding the critical suit and not the trump suit itself. In fact, any signal made about a suit in another suit might be called as such.

Advanced Bidding Techniques

Every call (including "pass", also sometimes called "no bid") serves two purposes. It confirms or passes some information to a partner, and also denies by implication any other kind of hand which would have tended to support an alternative call. For example, a bid of 2NT immediately after partner's 1NT not only shows a balanced hand of a certain point range, but also would almost always deny possession of a five-card major suit (otherwise the player would have bid it) or even a four card major suit (in that case, the player would probably have used the Stayman convention).

Likewise, in some partnerships the bid of 2♥ in the sequence 1NT– 2♣–2♦–2♥ between partners (opponents passing throughout) explicitly shows five hearts but also confirms four cards in spades: the bidder must hold at least five hearts to make it worth looking for a heart fit after 2♦ denied a four card major, and with at least five hearts, a Stayman bid must have been justified by having exactly four spades, the other major (since Stayman (as used by this partnership) is not useful with anything except a four card major suit). Thus an astute partner can read much more than the surface meaning into the bidding. Alternatively, many partnerships play this same bidding sequence as "Crawling Stayman" by which the responder shows a weak hand (less than eight high card points) with shortness in diamonds but at least four hearts and four spades; the opening bidder may correct to spades if that appears to be the better contract.

The situations detailed here are extremely simple examples; many instances of advanced bidding involve specific agreements related to very specific situations and subtle inferences regarding entire sequences of calls.

Play Techniques

Terence Reese, a prolific author of bridge books, points out that there are only four ways of taking a trick by force, two of which are very easy

- establishing long suits (the last cards in a suit will take tricks if the opponents don't have the suit and are unable to trump)

- playing a high card that no one else can beat

- playing for the opponents' high cards to be in a particular position (if their ace is to the right of your king, your king may be able to take a trick, especially if, when that suit is led, the player to your right has to play their card before you do)

- trumping an opponent's high card

Nearly all trick-taking techniques in bridge can be reduced to one of these four methods. The optimum play of the cards can require much thought and experience and is the subject of whole books on bridge.

Example:

The cards are dealt as shown in the bridge hand diagram; North is the dealer and starts the auction which proceeds as shown in the bidding table:

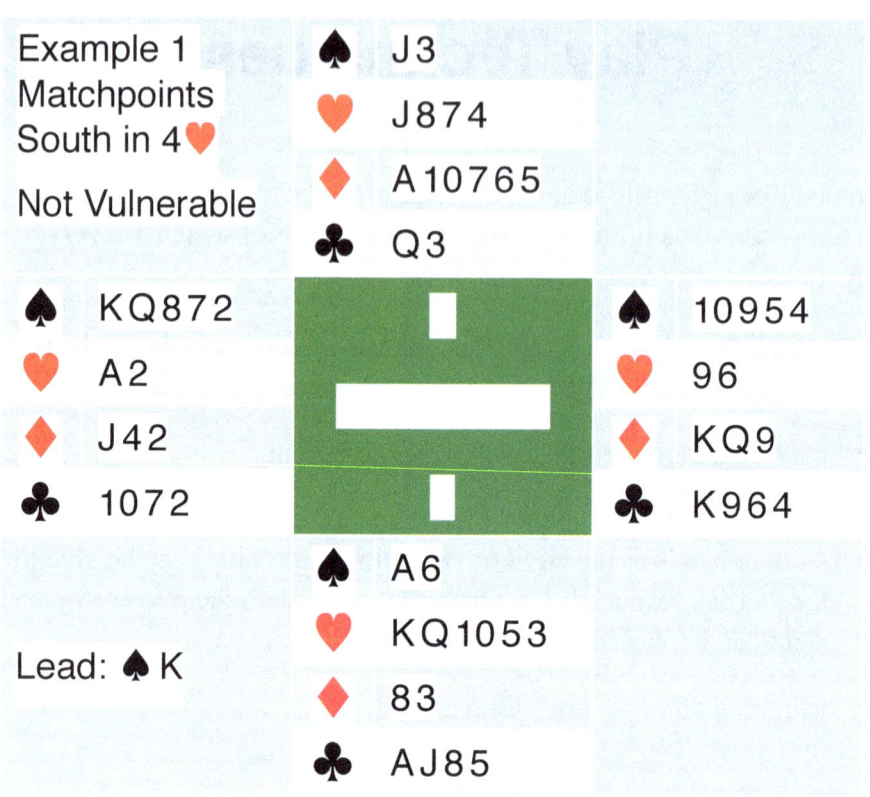

Example 1
Matchpoints
South in 4♥

Not Vulnerable

♠ J3
♥ J874
♦ A10765
♣ Q3

♠ KQ872
♥ A2
♦ J42
♣ 1072

♠ 10954
♥ 96
♦ KQ9
♣ K964

Lead: ♠ K

♠ A6
♥ KQ1053
♦ 83
♣ AJ85

West	North	East	South
	Pass	Pass	1♥
1♠	2♥	2♠	3♣
Pass	4♥	Pass	Pass
Pass			

As neither North nor East have sufficient strength to *open* the bidding, they each pass, denying such strength. South, next in turn, opens with the bid of 1♥, which denotes a reasonable heart suit (at least 4 or 5 cards long, depending on the bidding system) and at least 12 high card points. On this hand, South has 14 high card points. West *overcalls* with 1♠, since he has a long spade suit of reasonable quality and 10 high card points (an overcall can be made on a hand that is not quite strong enough for an opening bid). North *supports* partner's suit with 2♥, showing heart support and about 6–8 points. East supports spades with 2♠. South inserts a *game try* of 3♣, *inviting* the partner to bid the *game* of 4♥ with good club support and overall values. North complies, as North is at the higher end of the range for his 2♥ bid, and has a fourth trump (the 2♥ bid promised only three), and the *doubleton* queen of clubs to fit with partner's strength there. (North could instead have bid 3♥, indicating not enough strength for game, asking South to pass and so play 3♥.)

In the auction, north–south are trying to investigate whether their cards are sufficient to make a **game** (nine tricks at notrump, ten tricks in hearts or spades, 11 tricks in clubs or diamonds), which yields bonus points if bid and made. East-West are *competing* in spades, hoping to play a contract in spades at a low level. 4♥ is the final contract, 10 tricks being required for N-S to make with hearts as trump.

South is the *declarer*, having been first to bid hearts, and the player to South's left, West, has to choose the first card in the play, known as the *opening lead*. West chooses the spade king because spades is the suit the partnership has shown strength in, and because they have agreed that when they hold two *touching honors* (or *adjacent honors*) they will play the higher one first. West plays the card face down, to give their partner and the declarer (but not dummy) a chance to ask any last questions about the bidding or to object if they believe West is not the correct hand to lead. After that, North's cards are laid on the table and North becomes *dummy*, as both the North and South hands will be controlled by the declarer. West turns the lead card face up, and the declarer studies the two hands to make a plan for the play. On this hand, the trump ace, a spade, and a diamond trick must be lost, so declarer must not lose a trick in clubs.

If the ♣K is held by West, South will find it very hard to prevent it from making a trick (unless West leads a club). However, there is an almost-equal chance that it is held by East, in which case it can be 'trapped' against the ace, and will be beaten, using a tactic known as a *finesse*.

After considering the cards, the declarer directs dummy (North) to play a small spade. East plays *low* (small card) and South takes the ♠A, gaining the *lead*. (South may also elect to *duck*, but for the purpose of this example, let us assume South wins the ♠A at trick 1). South proceeds by *drawing trump*, leading the ♥K. West decides there is no benefit to holding back, and so wins the trick with the ace, and then cashes the ♠Q. For fear of conceding a *ruff and discard*, West plays the ♦2 instead of another spade. Declarer plays low from the table, and East scores the ♦Q. Not having anything better to do, East returns the remaining trump, taken in South's hand. The trumps now accounted for, South can now execute the finesse, perhaps trapping the king as planned. South *enters* the dummy (i.e. wins a trick in the dummy's hand) by leading a low diamond, using dummy's ♦A to win the trick, and leads the ♣Q from dummy to the next trick. East *covers* the queen with the king, and South takes the trick with the ace, and proceeds by *cashing* the remaining *master* ♣J. (If East doesn't play the king, then South will play a low club from South's hand and the queen will win anyway, this being the essence of the finesse). The game is now safe: South *ruffs* a small club with a dummy's trump, then ruffs a diamond in hand for an *entry* back, and ruffs the last club in dummy (sometimes described as a *crossruff*). Finally, South *claims* the remaining tricks by showing his or her hand, as it now contains only high trumps and there's no need to play the hand out to prove they are all winners.

(The trick-by-trick notation used above can be also expressed in tabular form, but a textual explanation is usually preferred in practice, for reader's convenience. Plays of small cards or *discards* are often omitted from such a description, unless they were important for the outcome).

North-South score the required 10 tricks, and their opponents take the remaining three. The contract is fulfilled, and North enters the pair numbers, the contract, and the score of +420 for the winning side (North is in charge of bookkeeping in duplicate tournaments) on the traveling sheet. North asks East to check the score entered on the traveller. All players return their own cards to the board, and the next deal is played.

On the prior hand, it is quite possible that the ♣K is held by West. For example, by swapping the ♣K and ♥A between the defending hands. Then the 4♥ contract would fail by one trick (unless West had led a club early in the play). However the failure of the contract would not mean that 4♥ is a bad contract on this hand. The contract depends on the club finesse working, or a mis-defense. The bonus points awarded for making a game contract far outweigh the penalty for going one off, so it is best strategy in the long run to bid game contracts such as this one.

Similarly, there is a minuscule chance that the ♣K is in the west hand, but the west hand has no other clubs. In that case, declarer can succeed by simply cashing the ♣A, felling the ♣K and setting up the ♣Q as a winner. However the chance of this is far lower than the simple chance of approximately 50% that East started with the ♣K. Therefore, the superior *percentage* play is to take the club finesse, as described above.

TRIK Source Code

TRIK 1.0 Listing

```
Name    : TRIK 1.0
Length  : $0BD9 (3033)

   5 IF MENU THEN 10:
     GOSUB 10000
  10 CLR:
     K = 0:
     L = 0:
     GOTO 500
 100 POKE 800,X MOD 256:
     POKE 801,X / 256:
     POKE 802,Y
 110 CALL 3761
 120 POKE 28,255
 130 CALL 3805
 140 PO = PO + 1
 300 X = X + 7:
     IF X <= 279 THEN 320:
     POP :
     GOTO 6000
 320 RETURN
 500 P = 0:
     POKE 806,1:
     POKE 807,0
 510 PO = 16400
 520 DIM N$(30)
1100 D$ = "<ctrl-D>":
     REM  "CTRL D"
1110 PRINT D$;"NOMON I,O,C"
1115 GOSUB 9000
1120 PRINT D$;"BLOAD ALPHASOFT"
1130 PRINT D$;"BLOAD LETTER-X"
1160 CAP = 0:
     X = 0:
     Y = 0
1180 K = PEEK (PO)
```

```
1187 IF K # 155 THEN 1190:
     CAP = 1:
     PO = PO + 1:
     GOTO 1180
1190 IF K < 219 AND K > 192 THEN 2000:
     REM  ALPHA
1195 IF K = 160 THEN 8000:
     REM  SPACE
1200 IF K < 186 AND K > 175 THEN 3000:
     REM  NUMBER
1220 IF K > 160 AND K < 193 THEN 4000:
     REM   SPECIAL
1240 IF K = 136 THEN 5000:
     REM  BACKSPACE
1260 IF K = 141 THEN 6000:
     REM  NEW LINE
1280 IF K = 129 THEN 7000:
     REM  NEW PAGE
1300 IF K = 130 THEN 7100:
     GOTO 1180
2000 IF CAP = 1 THEN L = (K - 193) * 26 + 4772
2010 IF CAP = 0 THEN L = (K - 193) * 26 + 4096
2020 CAP = 0
2040 POKE 804,L MOD 256:
     POKE 805,L / 256
2060 GOSUB 100
2080 GOTO 1180
3000 L = (K - 176) * 26 + 5448
3020 POKE 804,L MOD 256:
     POKE 805,L / 256
3060 GOSUB 100
3080 GOTO 1180
4000 L = 5708 * (K = 161) + 5734 * (K = 162) + 5760 * (K =
167) + 5786 * (K = 168) + 5812 * (K = 169) + 5838 * (K = 172)
+ 5864 * (K = 173)
4020 L = L + 5890 * (K = 174) + 5916 * (K = 186) + 5942 * (K
= 187) + 5968 * (K = 191)
4030 L = L + 6046 * (K = 163) + 6072 * (K = 164) + 6098 * (K
= 170) + 6124 * (K = 171) + 6150 * (K = 175) + 6176 * (K =
189) + 6202 * (K = 188) + 6228 * (K = 190)
4035 L = L + 6254 * (K = 192) + 6280 * (K = 166) + 6306 * (K
= 165)
4040 IF L = 0 THEN 1240
4060 POKE 804,L MOD 256:
     POKE 805,L / 256
4080 GOSUB 100
```

```
4100 GOTO 1180
5000 X = X - 7:
     IF X >= 0 THEN 5020
5010 X = 273:
     Y = Y - 8:
     IF Y < 0 THEN Y = 0
5020 POKE 800,X MOD 256:
     POKE 801,X / 256:
     POKE 802,Y:
     CALL 3761
5030 POKE 804,5994 MOD 256:
     POKE 805,5994 / 256
5040 POKE 28,0:
     CALL 3805
5045 PO = PO - 1
5050 GOTO 1180
6000 X = 0:
     Y = Y + 8
6010 POKE PO,141:
     PO = PO + 1
6020 IF Y > 183 THEN 7000
6040 GOTO 1180
7000 IF P = 5 THEN 7100
7010 X = 0:
     Y = 184:
     POKE 804,6020 MOD 256:
     POKE 805,6020 / 256:
     GOSUB 100
7012 CALL -198
7015 K = PEEK (-16384):
     IF K <= 127 THEN 7015:
     POKE -16368,0
7020 GOTO 1140
7100 X = 0:
     Y = 184:
     POKE 804,5994 MOD 256:
     POKE 805,5994 / 256:
     GOSUB 100
7120 K = PEEK (-16384):
     IF K <= 127 THEN 7120:
     POKE -16368,0
7140 IF K # ASC("1") AND K # ASC("2") THEN 7120
7160 IF K = ASC("1") THEN PRINT D$;"RUN TRIK 1.0 BID"
7180 PRINT D$;"RUN BUILD-A-HAND"
7200 END
8000 POKE PO,160:
```

```
      PO = PO + 1
8010 X = X + 7:
      IF X > 279 THEN 6000
8020 GOTO 1180
9000 PRINT D$;"BLOAD PCARD"
9010 CALL 3072:
      POKE -16302,0
9020 POKE 6635,0:
      POKE 6636,0:
      POKE 6637,65
9030 POKE 6638,13:
      POKE 6639,4:
      CALL 6650
9040 POKE 6635,50:
      POKE 6638,12:
      POKE 6639,3:
      CALL 6650
9050 POKE 6635,100:
      POKE 6638,11:
      POKE 6639,2:
      CALL 6650
9060 POKE 6635,150:
      POKE 6638,10:
      POKE 6639,1:
      CALL 6650
9070 POKE 6635,200:
      POKE 6638,9:
      POKE 6639,4:
      CALL 6650
9080 RETURN
10000 STROBE = -16368:
      HOME = -936:
      INV = -384:
      NML = -380:
      CALL INV:
      TEXT:
      CALL HOME
10010 VTAB 1:
      TAB 2:
      PRINT "    ";:
      TAB 9:
      PRINT "     ";:
      TAB 17:
      PRINT "    ";:
      TAB 25:
      PRINT " ";:
```

```
      TAB 33:
      PRINT "         "
10020 PRINT " ";:
      TAB 5:
      PRINT " ";:
      TAB 9:
      PRINT " ";:
      TAB 13:
      PRINT " ";:
      TAB 17:
      PRINT " ";:
      TAB 21:
      PRINT " ";:
      TAB 25:
      PRINT " ";:
      TAB 33:
      PRINT " "
10030 PRINT "        ";::
      TAB 9:
      PRINT "       ";::
      TAB 17:
      PRINT "       ";::
      TAB 25:
      PRINT " ";:
      TAB 33:
      PRINT "      "
10040 PRINT " ";:
      TAB 5:
      PRINT " ";:
      TAB 9:
      PRINT " ";:
      TAB 17:
      PRINT " ";:
      TAB 25:
      PRINT " ";:
      TAB 33:
      PRINT " "
10050 PRINT " ";:
      TAB 5:
      PRINT " ";:
      TAB 7:
      PRINT " ";:
      TAB 9:
      PRINT " ";:
      TAB 15:
      PRINT " ";:
```

```
      TAB 17:
      PRINT " ";
10060 TAB 23:
      PRINT " ";:
      TAB 25:
      PRINT "       ";:
      TAB 31:
      PRINT " ";:
      TAB 33:
      PRINT "      ";:
      TAB 39:
      PRINT " "
10070 CALL NML:
      PRINT
10080 PRINT "A       P       P       L       E":
      TAB 2:
      PRINT "P       U       R       I       X"
10090 TAB 3:
      PRINT "P       G       O       B       C":
      TAB 4:
      PRINT "L       E       G       R       H"
10100 TAB 5:
      PRINT "E       T       R       A       A":
      TAB 14:
      PRINT "S       A       R       N"
10110 TAB 15:
      PRINT "O       M       Y       G":
      TAB 16:
      PRINT "U";:
      TAB 40:
      PRINT "E";
10120 TAB 17:
      PRINT "N":
      TAB 18:
      PRINT "D"
10130 CALL INV:
      PRINT:
      PRINT:
      TAB 10:
      PRINT "                   ":
      TAB 10:
      PRINT "  P R E S E N T S  ":
      TAB 10:
      PRINT "                   "
10140 CALL NML:
      FOR I = 1 TO 1200:
```

48

```
      NEXT I
11000 IL = -1:
      DIM R$(4), SP$(28):
      SP$ = "                          ":
      FOR I = 1 TO 9:
      PRINT "<ctrl-J>":
      NEXT I:
      VTAB 12
11010 POKE 32,5:
      POKE 33,34:
      PRINT:
      CALL INV:
      PRINT SP$:
      PRINT "   A.P.P.L.E.  DISKPAK 7B   ":
      PRINT SP$:
      PRINT "  TRIK 1.0 BY JAMES HILGER  "
11020 PRINT SP$:
      CALL NML:
      PRINT:
      TEXT:
      POKE 37,PEEK (37) - 6:
      RETURN
```

TRIK 1.0 BID Listing

```
Name    : TRIK 1.0 BID
Length  : $43FB (17403)

     0 CLR
    10 POKE -16298,0:
       TEXT:
       CALL -936
    20 DIM DEAL(52),VAL(13),PLAY(52),SUIT(16),OUT(16)
    22 P = M = LEDL = LEDH = MTCH = H = I = TRL = TRH = DM13 =
TEMP = Q
    30 DIM DCS(5)
    40 DIM XX$(4), CTR$(2)
    50 DIM GAME(5):
       GAME(1) = 5:
       GAME(2) = 5:
       GAME(3) = 4:
       GAME(4) = 4:
       GAME(5) = 3
   100 DIM SUCNT(16),HCNT(4),SURK(16)
   103 DIM TAL(16), SS$(10)
   105 DIM OPB(4),MAX(4),SUBID(16)
   110 DIM RK$(52), SU$(52)
   115 DIM R(4), BID$(76)
   120 RK$ =
"23456789TJQKA23456789TJQKA23456789TJQKA23456789TJQKA"
   130 SU$ =
"CCCCCCCCCCCCCCDDDDDDDDDDDDDDDHHHHHHHHHHHHHHHSSSSSSSSSSSSSS"
   136 BID$ =
"PADBRD1C1D1H1S1N2C2D2H2S2N3C3D3H3S3N4C4D4H4S4N5C5D5H5S5N6C6D6
H6S6N7C7D7H7S7N"
   140 CALL -936:
       FOR P = 1 TO 52:
       DEAL(P) = P:
       NEXT P:
       RE = 0
   150 FOR P = 1 TO 16:
       SUCNT(P) = 0:
       SURK(P) = 0:
       NEXT P
   160 FOR P = 1 TO 4:
       HCNT(P) = 0:
       NEXT P
   200 GR :
```

```
    PRINT:
    PRINT:
    COLOR=4
210 FOR I = 0 TO 39:
    VLIN 0,39 AT I:
    NEXT I
215 COLOR=15:
    FOR I = 23 TO 31:
    HLIN2,37 AT I:
    NEXT I
220 COLOR=12
225 VLIN 9,15 AT 2:
    VLIN 9,15 AT 3:
    VLIN 9,15 AT 5:
    VLIN 9,11 AT 6:
    VLIN 13,15 AT 6:
    VLIN 9,10 AT 4:
    VLIN 14,15 AT 4:
    PLOT4,12
230 VLIN 9,15 AT 8:
    VLIN 9,15 AT 9:
    VLIN 9,10 AT 10:
    VLIN 12,13 AT 10:
    VLIN 9,15 AT 11:
    VLIN 9,11 AT 12:
    VLIN 13,15 AT 12
235 VLIN 9,15 AT 15:
    VLIN 9,15 AT 16:
    VLIN 9,15 AT 17
240 VLIN 9,15 AT 20:
    VLIN 9,15 AT 21:
    VLIN 9,10 AT 22:
    VLIN 14,15 AT 22:
    VLIN 9,15 AT 23:
    VLIN 10,14 AT 24
245 VLIN 9,15 AT 26:
    VLIN 9,15 AT 27:
    HLIN28,30 AT 9:
    HLIN28,30 AT 10:
    HLIN28,30 AT 12:
    HLIN29,30 AT 13:
    HLIN28,30 AT 14:
    HLIN28,30 AT 15
250 HLIN32,36 AT 9:
    HLIN32,36 AT 10:
    HLIN32,33 AT 11:
```

```
    HLIN32,35 AT 12:
    HLIN32,33 AT 13:
    HLIN32,36 AT 14:
    HLIN32,36 AT 15
252 VLIN 0,39 AT 0:
    VLIN 0,39 AT 39:
    HLIN0,39 AT 0:
    HLIN0,39 AT 39
255 COLOR=0:
    VLIN 27,29 AT 3:
    VLIN 26,29 AT 4:
    VLIN 25,28 AT 5:
    VLIN 24,30 AT 6:
    VLIN 25,28 AT 7:
    VLIN 26,29 AT 8:
    VLIN 27,29 AT 9
260 COLOR=9:
    VLIN 24,27 AT 12:
    VLIN 24,28 AT 13:
    VLIN 24,29 AT 14:
    VLIN 26,30 AT 15:
    VLIN 24,29 AT 16:
    VLIN 24,28 AT 17:
    VLIN 24,27 AT 18
265 VLIN 25,29 AT 23:
    VLIN 24,30 AT 24:
    VLIN 25,29 AT 25:
    HLIN22,26 AT 26:
    HLIN21,27 AT 27:
    HLIN22,26 AT 28
270 COLOR=0:
    VLIN 27,30 AT 30:
    VLIN 27,30 AT 31:
    VLIN 27,30 AT 35:
    VLIN 27,30 AT 36:
    HLIN32,34 AT 24:
    HLIN32,34 AT 25:
    HLIN32,34 AT 26
271 VLIN 28,29 AT 32:
    VLIN 28,29 AT 34
275 VLIN 26,30 AT 33
900 CALL -936:
    PRINT
905 D$ = "<ctrl-D>":
    REM  CNTL D IN QUOTES
910 DLR = 0
```

```
 920 TAB 8:
     INPUT "DUPLICATE PLAY? (Y/N):",A$:
     IF A$="N" THEN 990:
     IF A$#"Y" THEN 900
 930 CALL -936:
     PRINT:
     TAB 8:
     INPUT "SAVED HAND NUMBER    ",HN
 940 PRINT D$;"OPEN HAND ";HN
 945 PRINT D$;"READ HAND ";HN
 950 FOR I = 1 TO 52:
     INPUT DEAL(I):
     NEXT I:
     INPUT DLR:
     INPUT VUL
 960 PRINT D$;"CLOSE HAND ";HN
 970 GOTO 1100
 990 CALL -936:
     PRINT
1000 REM  SHUFFLE
1005 PRINT:
     TAB 5:
     PRINT "YOUR HAND WILL BE DISPLAYED...":
     CALL -198
1010 FOR P = 1 TO 150:
     I = RND (52) + 1:
     J = RND (52) + 1:
     TEMP = DEAL(I):
     DEAL(I) = DEAL(J):
     DEAL(J) = TEMP
1017 NEXT P
1018 CALL -198:
     VUL = RND (20) MOD 2
1020 CALL -936:
     PRINT:
     TAB 4:
     PRINT "THE COMPUTER WILL BID THE OTHER":
     TAB 14:
     PRINT "THREE HANDS."
1025 RSP = 0:
     RSP2 = 0:
     DBL = 0
1027 D$ = "<ctrl-D>"
1030 FOR H = 1 TO 4
1040 FOR C = 1 TO 12
1050 I = C + (H - 1) * 13
```

```
1055 FOR J = I + 1 TO H * 13
1060 IF DEAL(I) > DEAL(J) THEN 1075
1070 TEMP = DEAL(I):
     DEAL(I) = DEAL(J):
     DEAL(J) = TEMP
1075 NEXT J
1080 NEXT C
1090 NEXT H
1100 TEXT
1200 CALL -936:
     PRINT "YOUR HAND LOOKS LIKE THIS:":
     PRINT:
     CALL -384:
     TAB 7:
     PRINT "SOUTH";:
     CALL -380
1205 IF VUL = 0 THEN PRINT " NOT VULNERABLE":
     IF VUL = 1 THEN PRINT " VULNERABLE"
1210 PRINT:
     ST = 27:
     GOSUB 2000
1215 IF RE # 1 THEN 1220:
     RSP = 0:
     RSP2 = 0:
     DBL = 0:
     PRINT:
     PRINT "YOUR COUNT IS ";HCNT(3);"   (REBID)":
     GOTO 1230
1220 GOSUB 2500
1230 GOSUB 3000
1232 VTAB 23:
     L1 = (LBID MOD 100) / 10:
     S1 = LBID MOD 10:
     IX = ((L1 - 1) * 5 + S1) * 2 + 5:
     IF L1 = 0 THEN IX = 1
1235 PRINT "CONTRACT: ";BID$(IX,IX + 1);" ";
1238 IF DBL = 0 THEN XX$ = "     ":
     IF DBL = 1 THEN XX$ = "DBL ":
     IF DBL = 2 THEN XX$ = "RDBL"
1240 PRINT XX$:
     VTAB 23:
     TAB 28:
     INPUT "HIT RETURN ",A$
1260 CALL -936
1265 VTAB 5:
     TAB 5:
```

```
      PRINT "CONTRACT: ";BID$(IX,IX + 1);" ";
1267 IF DBL = 0 THEN XX$ = "    ":
     IF DBL = 1 THEN XX$ = "DBL ":
     IF DBL = 2 THEN XX$ = "RDBL"
1268 PRINT XX$;:
     IF VUL = 0 THEN PRINT " NOT VULNERABLE":
     IF VUL = 1 THEN PRINT " VULNERABLE"
1270 VTAB 10:
     TAB 5:
     PRINT "1 -- DISPLAY THE HANDS":
     TAB 5:
     PRINT "2 -- PLAY OUT THE HANDS"
1280 TAB 5:
     PRINT "3 -- REBID THE SAME HANDS":
     TAB 5:
     PRINT "4 -- GET A NEW DEAL"
1285 TAB 5:
     PRINT "5 -- END"
1290 PRINT:
     PRINT:
     PRINT:
     TAB 15:
     PRINT "ENTER YOUR CHOICE."
1295 K = PEEK (-16384):
     IF K <= 127 THEN 1295:
     POKE -16368,0:
     IF K < 177 OR K > 181 THEN 1295:
     CHOICE = K - 176
1300 IF CHOICE = 1 THEN 1700
1320 IF CHOICE = 2 THEN 1400
1340 IF CHOICE = 3 THEN 1500
1360 IF CHOICE = 4 THEN 140
1365 CALL -936
1370 END
1400 CALL -936
1405 PRINT D$;"NOMON C,I,O"
1410 CTR$ = BID$(IX,IX + 1)
1420 CALL -936
1450 PRINT D$;"CHAIN TRIK 1.0 PLAY"
1500 RE = 1:
     GOTO 1200
1700 CALL -936
1750 POKE 32,6
1790 PRINT
1800 ST = 1:
     GOSUB 2000
```

```
1805 POKE 32,8:
     PRINT
1810 ST = 14:
     GOSUB 2000
1815 POKE 32,6:
     PRINT
1820 ST = 27:
     GOSUB 2000
1825 POKE 32,8:
     PRINT
1830 ST = 40:
     GOSUB 2000
1840 CALL -384
1845 POKE 32,0
1850 VTAB 3:
     PRINT "NORTH"
1860 VTAB 8:
     PRINT "EAST"
1870 VTAB 13:
     PRINT "SOUTH"
1880 VTAB 18:
     PRINT "WEST"
1885 CALL -380
1890 VTAB 23:
     INPUT "HIT RETURN ",A$
1900 GOTO 1260
2000 PRINT "SPADES:   ";
2010 CALL -384:
     FOR P = ST TO ST + 12
2015 IF DEAL(P) <= 39 THEN 2030
2020 IF RK$(DEAL(P),DEAL(P))#"T" THEN 2025:
     PRINT "10 ";:
     GOTO 2030
2025 PRINT RK$(DEAL(P),DEAL(P));" ";
2030 NEXT P:
     CALL -380:
     PRINT ""
2040 PRINT "HEARTS:   ";
2050 CALL -384:
     FOR P = ST TO ST + 12
2055 IF DEAL(P) >= 40 OR DEAL(P) <= 26 THEN 2070
2060 IF RK$(DEAL(P),DEAL(P))#"T" THEN 2065:
     PRINT "10 ";:
     GOTO 2070
2065 PRINT RK$(DEAL(P),DEAL(P));" ";
2070 NEXT P:
```

```
      CALL -380:
      PRINT ""
 2080 PRINT "DIAMONDS:";
 2090 CALL -384:
      FOR P = ST TO ST + 12
 2095 IF DEAL(P) >= 27 OR DEAL(P) <= 13 THEN 2110
 2100 IF RK$(DEAL(P),DEAL(P))#"T" THEN 2105:
      PRINT "10 ";:
      GOTO 2110
 2105 PRINT RK$(DEAL(P),DEAL(P));" ";
 2110 NEXT P:
      CALL -380:
      PRINT ""
 2120 PRINT "CLUBS:    ";
 2130 CALL -384:
      FOR P = ST TO ST + 12
 2135 IF DEAL(P) >= 14 THEN 2150
 2140 IF RK$(DEAL(P),DEAL(P))#"T" THEN 2145:
      PRINT "10 ";:
      GOTO 2150
 2145 PRINT RK$(DEAL(P),DEAL(P));" ";
 2150 NEXT P:
      CALL -380:
      PRINT ""
 2160 RETURN
 2500 FOR H = 1 TO 4:
      K = (H - 1) * 4
 2510 FOR C = 1 TO 13:
      I = C + (H - 1) * 13
 2520 IF DEAL(I) > 39 THEN SUCNT(1 + K) = SUCNT(1 + K) + 1
 2530 IF DEAL(I) < 40 AND DEAL(I) > 26 THEN SUCNT(2 + K) =
SUCNT(2 + K) + 1
 2540 IF DEAL(I) < 27 AND DEAL(I) > 13 THEN SUCNT(3 + K) =
SUCNT(3 + K) + 1
 2550 IF DEAL(I) < 14 THEN SUCNT(4 + K) = SUCNT(4 + K) + 1
 2560 IF DEAL(I) MOD 13 # 0 THEN 2570
 2563 RANK = 4
 2565 HCNT(H) = HCNT(H) + 4
 2568 GOSUB 10500
 2570 IF (DEAL(I) + 1) MOD 13 # 0 THEN 2580
 2573 RANK = 3
 2575 HCNT(H) = HCNT(H) + 3
 2578 GOSUB 10500
 2580 IF (DEAL(I) + 2) MOD 13 # 0 THEN 2590
 2583 RANK = 2
 2585 HCNT(H) = HCNT(H) + 2
```

```
2588 GOSUB 10500
2590 IF (DEAL(I) + 3) MOD 13 # 0 THEN 2600
2593 RANK = 1
2595 HCNT(H) = HCNT(H) + 1
2598 GOSUB 10500
2600 NEXT C
2610 FOR P = 1 TO 4
2620 IF SUCNT(P + K) = 0 THEN HCNT(H) = HCNT(H) + 3
2630 IF SUCNT(P + K) = 1 THEN HCNT(H) = HCNT(H) + 2
2640 IF SUCNT(P + K) = 2 THEN HCNT(H) = HCNT(H) + 1
2650 NEXT P:
     NEXT H
2660 PRINT:
     PRINT "YOUR COUNT IS ";HCNT(3)
2670 FOR H = 1 TO 4:
     FOR P = 1 TO 4 :
2680 BS = (H - 1) * 4 + P
2690 TAL(BS) = 5 * (SUCNT(BS) > 3) * (SUCNT(BS) - 2) +
SURK(BS)
2700 NEXT P,H
2750 RETURN
3000 REM  BIDDING CONTROL ROUTINE
3010 PRINT:
     PRINT "BIDDING:":
     PRINT "-------------------------------------"
3020 PRINT
3025 CALL -384:
     VTAB 15:
     TAB 17:
     PRINT "NORTH":
     VTAB 18:
     TAB 5:
     PRINT "WEST":
     VTAB 18:
     TAB 30:
     PRINT "EAST":
     VTAB 21:
     TAB 17:
     PRINT "SOUTH":
     CALL -380
3030 LBID = 0:
     PCNT = 0:
     FOR I = 1 TO 4:
     OPB(I) = 0:
     MAX(I) = 0:
     R(I) = 0:
```

```
      NEXT I:
      FOR I = 1 TO 16:
      SUBID(I) = 0:
      NEXT I
 3031 BWD = 0:
      FOR I = 1 TO 5:
      DCS(I) = 0:
      NEXT I
 3032 IF DLR = 0 THEN 3033:
      Q = DLR:
      RSP = 0:
      RSP2 = 0:
      DBL = 0:
      GOTO 3040
 3033 IF RE # 1 THEN 3035:
      RE = 0:
      GOTO 3040
 3035 Q = RND (4) + 1
 3040 FOR I = 1 TO 4
 3060 H = Q - 1 + I:
      IF H > 4 THEN H = H - 4
 3065 L1 = 0:
      S1 = 0
 3070 R(H) = R(H) + 1
 3075 PH = H + 2:
      IF PH > 4 THEN PH = PH - 4
 3080 IF H # 3 THEN 3090:
      GOSUB 9000:
      GOTO 3350
 3090 IF BWD > 0 AND OPB(H) > 10 THEN GOSUB 17000
 3095 IF L1 = 0 THEN 3100:
      GOSUB 10600:
      GOTO 3400
 3100 IF HCNT(H) > 12 AND LBID = 0 THEN GOSUB 3500
 3110 IF L1 = 0 THEN 3120:
      GOSUB 10600:
      GOTO 3400
 3120 IF OPB(H) > 107 THEN GOSUB 4000
 3130 IF L1 = 0 THEN 3140:
      GOSUB 10600:
      GOTO 3400
 3140 IF OPB(H) = 0 AND R(H) = 1 AND HCNT(H) < 10 THEN GOSUB
4500
 3150 IF L1 = 0 THEN 3160:
      GOSUB 10600:
      GOTO 3400
```

```
 3160 IF R(PH) = 1 AND (OPB(H) MOD 100) / 10 = 3 AND OPB(PH) <
100 THEN GOSUB 5000
 3170 IF L1 = 0 THEN 3180:
      GOSUB 10600:
      GOTO 3400
 3180 IF LBID > 106 AND OPB(H) = 0 AND R(H) = 1 AND HCNT(H) >
12 THEN GOSUB 5500
 3190 IF L1 = 0 THEN 3200:
      GOSUB 10600:
      GOTO 3400
 3200 IF OPB(H) = 106 THEN GOSUB 6000
 3210 IF L1 = 0 THEN 3220:
      GOSUB 10600:
      GOTO 3400
 3220 IF R(H) = 1 AND LBID # 0 AND OPB(H) = 0 THEN GOSUB 6500
 3230 IF L1 = 0 THEN 3240:
      GOSUB 10600:
      GOTO 3400
 3240 IF R(PH) = 1 AND OPB(H) # 0 AND OPB(H) < 100 AND OPB(PH)
< 100 THEN GOSUB 7000
 3250 IF L1 = 0 THEN 3260:
      GOSUB 10600:
      GOTO 3400
 3260 IF OPB(PH) > 106 OR OPB(PH) = 106 AND OPB(H) > 0 THEN
GOSUB 7500
 3270 IF L1 = 0 THEN 3274:
      GOSUB 10600:
      GOTO 3400
 3274 IF R(PH) = 2 AND (RSP = H OR RSP2 = H) THEN GOSUB 5600
 3276 IF L1 = 0 THEN 3280:
      GOSUB 10600:
      GOTO 3400
 3280 IF OPB(PH) > 10 THEN GOSUB 8000
 3290 IF L1 = 0 THEN 3293:
      GOSUB 10600:
      GOTO 3400
 3293 IF H = 2 OR H = 4 THEN GOSUB 15000
 3294 IF L1 = 0 THEN 3300:
      GOSUB 10600:
      GOTO 3400
 3300 GOSUB 9500:
      PCNT = PCNT + 1
 3350 IF LBID = 0 AND PCNT = 4 THEN I = 4
 3360 IF LBID > 0 AND PCNT = 3 THEN I = 4
 3400 NEXT I
 3420 IF LBID = 0 AND PCNT = 4 THEN 3490
```

```
3430 IF LBID > 0 AND PCNT = 3 THEN 3490
3440 GOTO 3040
3490 RETURN
3500 REM  OPEN ROUTINE
3510 GOSUB 11000
3560 IF HCNT(H) > 15 THEN 3600
3570 IF S1 # 0 THEN 3580:
     S1 = 101:
     L1 = 1:
     MAX(H) = 13:
     GOTO 3980
3580 S1 = S1 + 100:
     L1 = 1:
     MAX(H) = 14:
     GOTO 3980
3600 REM  POINTS > 15
3605 NH = (H - 1) * 4
3610 NT = 1:
     FOR P = 1 TO 4
3620 IF SUCNT(NH + P) < 2 THEN NT = 0
3625 IF SUCNT(NH + P) > 5 THEN NT = 0
3630 IF SUCNT(NH + P) + SURK(NH + P) < 5 THEN NT = 0
3640 NEXT P
3650 IF NT = 0 THEN 3700
3660 IF HCNT(H) > 18 THEN 3670:
     S1 = 105:
     L1 = 1:
     MAX(H) = 18:
     GOTO 3980
3670 IF HCNT(H) > 21 THEN 3680:
     GOTO 3570
3680 IF HCNT(H) > 24 THEN 3690:
     S1 = 105:
     L1 = 2:
     MAX(H) = 24:
     GOTO 3980
3690 S1 = 105:
     L1 = 3:
     MAX(H) = 27:
     GOTO 3980
3700 REM  NOT NT
3710 IF HCNT(H) < 21 THEN 3570
3720 S1 = S1 + 100:
     L1 = 2:
     MAX(H) = 21:
     GOTO 3980
```

```
3980 RETURN
4000 REM  RESPOND TO OPEN
4010 RSP = H
4015 IF DBL # 1 THEN 4020:
     IF HCNT(H) < 10 THEN 4020:
     MAX(H) = 12:
     L1 = 1:
     S1 = 7:
     GOTO 4490
4020 PS = OPB(H) MOD 10
4030 IF PS = 5 THEN 4480
4035 IF OPB(H) MOD 100 = 11 THEN 4200
4040 GOSUB 13000:
     IF S1 = 0 THEN 4200
4050 IF (OPB(H) MOD 100) / 10 > 1 THEN 4100
4060 IF HCNT(H) < 7 THEN 4200
4070 GOSUB 14000
4075 IF HCNT(H) > 10 THEN 4080:
     MAX(H) = 10:
     GOTO 4490
4080 IF HCNT(H) < 13 THEN 4200
4085 IF HCNT(H) > 16 THEN 4200:
     L1 = L1 + 1:
     MAX(H) = 16:
     GOTO 4490
4100 IF HCNT(H) > 6 THEN 4120:
     S1 = 5:
     GOSUB 14000:
     MAX(H) = 6:
     GOTO 4490
4120 GOSUB 14000:
     MAX(H) = 10:
     GOTO 4490
4200 REM  BID A NEW SUIT
4205 L1 = 0
4210 IF (OPB(H) MOD 100) / 10 > 1 THEN 4350
4220 IF HCNT(H) < 6 THEN 4490
4230 GOSUB 11000
4240 IF S1 = 0 THEN 4260
4245 GOSUB 14000:
     IF HCNT(H) < 10 AND L1 > 1 THEN 4250:
     IF HCNT(H) > 18 THEN 4255:
     IF L1 = 1 THEN 4248:
     MAX(H) = 10:
     GOTO 4490
4248 MAX(H) = 6:
```

63

```
        GOTO 4490
 4250 L1 = 0:
        GOTO 4490
 4255 MAX(H) = 19:
        L1 = L1 + 1:
        GOTO 4490
 4260 NH = (H - 1) * 4
 4265 NT = 1:
        FOR P = 1 TO 4
 4267 IF PS = 5 - P THEN 4285
 4270 IF SUCNT(NH + P) < 2 THEN NT = 0
 4275 IF SUCNT(NH + P) > 5 THEN NT = 0
 4280 IF SUCNT(NH + P) + SURK(NH + P) < 5 AND SUCNT(NH + P) <
3 THEN NT = 0
 4285 NEXT P
 4290 IF NT = 0 THEN 4490
 4295 S1 = 5:
        GOSUB 14000:
        IF HCNT(H) > 10 THEN 4310
 4300 MAX(H) = 10:
        GOTO 4490
 4310 IF HCNT(H) > 15 THEN 4320:
        MAX(H) = 15:
        L1 = L1 + 1:
        IF L1 > 2 THEN L1 = L1 - 1:
        GOTO 4490
 4320 MAX(H) = 18:
        L1 = L1 + 2:
        IF L1 > 3 THEN L1 = L1 - 1:
        GOTO 4490
 4350 IF HCNT(H) > 6 THEN 4370
 4360 S1 = 5:
        GOSUB 14000:
        MAX(H) = 6:
        GOTO 4490
 4370 GOSUB 11000:
        IF S1 = 0 THEN S1 = 5:
        IF S1 = 5 THEN MAX(H) = 6:
        IF S1 # 5 THEN MAX(H) = 9
 4380 GOSUB 14000:
        GOTO 4490
 4480 IF HCNT(H) < 7 THEN 4490:
        S1 = 5:
        MAX(H) = 9:
        GOSUB 14000:
        IF HCNT(H) < 10 THEN 4490
```

```
 4485 L1 = L1 + 1:
      MAX(H) = 14
 4490 IF L1 > 7 THEN L1 = 0:
      RETURN
 4500 REM   PREEMPT
 4505 IF VUL = 1 THEN 4990
 4510 IF (LBID MOD 100) / 10 > 2 THEN 4990
 4540 S1 = 0:
      FOR P = 1 TO 4:
      IF SUCNT((H - 1) * 4 + 5 - P) > 6 AND SURK((H - 1) * 4 +
5 - P) > 2 THEN S1 = P:
      NEXT P
 4560 IF S1 = 0 THEN 4990
 4580 MAX(H) = 10:
      L1 = 3
 4990 RETURN
 5000 REM   PREEMPT RESPONSE
 5010 PS = OPB(H) MOD 10:
      IF HCNT(H) < 12 THEN 5490
 5020 IF SUCNT((H - 1) * 4 + 5 - PS) < 1 THEN 5490
 5040 S1 = PS:
      GOSUB 14000
 5060 GOTO 5490
 5490 RETURN
 5500 REM   TAKE OUT DBL
 5510 MAX(H) = 15:
      L1 = 1:
      S1 = 106
 5520 RETURN
 5600 REM   REBID BY RESPONDER
 5602 IF MAX(PH) + HCNT(H) > 31 AND (LBID MOD 100) / 10 < 6
THEN 5605
 5603 IF OPB(H) = 51 OR OPB(H) = 52 OR OPB(H) = 43 OR OPB(H) =
44 OR OPB(H) = 35 THEN 5990
 5605 PS = OPB(H) MOD 10:
      FS = OPB(PH) MOD 10:
      IF PS = 0 OR FS = 0 THEN 5990
 5607 BB = 0:
      FOR P = 1 TO 4:
      IF SUBID((H - 1) * 4 + 5 - P) > 0 AND SUBID((PH - 1) * 4
+ 5 - P) > 0 THEN BB = P:
      NEXT P
 5609 NB = 0:
      FOR P = 1 TO 4:
```

```
      IF SUBID((PH - 1) * 4 + 5 - P) > 0 AND BB # P AND
SUCNT((H - 1) * 4 + 5 - P) > 2 AND SURK((H - 1) * 4 + 5 - P) >
1 THEN NB = P:
      NEXT P
 5610 IF FS = 5 OR FS = 7 THEN 5613
 5612 RBS = 0:
      IF SUCNT((H - 1) * 4 + 5 - FS) > 5 THEN RBS = FS
 5613 GOSUB 13000:
      IF S1 = BB OR S1 = NB THEN S1 = 0:
      MB = S1
 5614 GOSUB 12000:
      IF S1 = BB OR S1 = NB THEN S1 = 0
 5615 IF HCNT(H) > 9 THEN 5700
 5620 MAX(H) = 9:
      IF HCNT(H) < 8 AND MAX(PH) < 16 THEN 5990
 5630 IF BB < 3 THEN 5640:
      S1 = BB:
      GOSUB 14000:
      GOTO 5990
 5640 IF NB < 3 THEN 5650:
      S1 = NB:
      GOSUB 14000:
      GOTO 5990
 5650 IF RBS < 3 THEN 5655:
      S1 = RBS:
      GOSUB 14000:
      GOTO 5990
 5655 IF MB = 0 THEN 5660:
      S1 = MB:
      GOSUB 14000:
      GOTO 5990
 5660 IF BB = 0 THEN 5670:
      S1 = BB:
      GOSUB 14000:
      GOTO 5990
 5670 IF NB = 0 THEN 5680:
      S1 = NB:
      GOSUB 14000:
      GOTO 5990
 5680 IF RBS = 0 THEN 5690:
      S1 = RBS:
      GOSUB 14000:
      GOTO 5990
 5690 IF S1 = 0 THEN S1 = 5:
      GOSUB 14000:
      IF L1 > 2 AND MAX(PH) < 16 THEN L1 = 0:
```

```
      GOTO 5990
 5700 IF HCNT(H) > 12 THEN 5800
 5710 MAX(H) = 12:
      GOTO 5630
 5800 IF HCNT(H) > 16 THEN 5900
 5810 MAX(H) = 16:
      GOTO 5630
 5900 NT = 1:
      FOR P = 1 TO 4:
      IF SUCNT((H - 1) * 4 + 5 - P) < 2 OR SUCNT((H - 1) * 4 +
5 - P) > 5 THEN NT = 0:
      NEXT P
 5910 IF NT = 0 THEN 5630:
      S1 = 5:
      GOSUB 14000:
      IF L1 < 3 THEN L1 = 3:
      IF L1 > 3 THEN 5920:
      GOTO 5990
 5920 L1 = 0:
      GOTO 5630
 5990 IF L1 = 0 THEN 5995:
      IF L1 > (HCNT(H) + MAX(PH)) / 6 THEN L1 = 0
 5995 RETURN
 6000 REM  T.O. DBL RESP
 6010 IF HCNT(H) > 5 THEN 6015:
      MAX(H) = 5:
      GOTO 6490
 6015 RSP2 = H
 6020 MAX(H) = 9:
      GOSUB 11000:
      IF S1 = 0 THEN 6050:
      GOSUB 14000
 6030 IF HCNT(H) < 13 THEN 6490:
      L1 = L1 + 1:
      MAX(H) = 13:
      GOTO 6490
 6050 S1 = 5:
      GOSUB 14000:
      GOTO 6490
 6490 RETURN
 6500 REM  OVERCALL
 6520 GOSUB 11000:
      IF S1 = 0 THEN 6560
 6540 IF SUCNT((H - 1) * 4 + 5 - S1) < 6 OR SURK((H - 1) * 4 +
5 - S1) < 4 THEN 6560
 6550 GOSUB 14000:
```

```
      GOTO 6990
 6560 IF HCNT(H) < 16 THEN 6990
 6580 NT = 1:
      FOR P = 1 TO 4:
      IF SUCNT((H - 1) * 4 + 5 - P) < 2 + SURK((H - 1) * 4 + 5
- P) < 5 THEN NT = 0:
      IF SUCNT((H - 1) * 4 + 5 - P) < 2 THEN NT = 0
 6600 IF SUCNT((H - 1) * 4 + 5 - P) > 5 THEN NT = 0:
      NEXT P
 6620 IF NT = 0 THEN 6990:
      S1 = 5:
      GOSUB 14000:
      IF L1 > 1 THEN L1 = 0:
      GOTO 6990
 6990 RETURN
 7000 REM  OVERCALL RESPONSE
 7020 PS = OPB(H) MOD 10:
      IF PS = 5 THEN 7300
 7040 IF HCNT(H) < 13 OR SUCNT((H - 1) * 4 + 5 - PS) < 2 THEN
7490
 7050 IF SUCNT((H - 1) * 4 + 5 - PS) = 2 AND SURK((H - 1) * 4
+ 5 - PS) = 0 THEN 7490
 7080 S1 = PS:
      GOSUB 14000
 7100 IF L1 < 4 THEN 7120:
      L1 = 0:
      GOTO 7490
 7120 IF S1 = 1 THEN L1 = 5
 7130 IF S1 = 2 THEN L1 = 5
 7140 IF S1 = 3 THEN L1 = 4
 7150 IF S1 = 4 THEN L1 = 4
 7160 GOTO 7490
 7300 IF HCNT(H) < 10 THEN 7490
 7320 S1 = 5:
      GOSUB 14000:
      IF L1 < 3 THEN 7340:
      L1 = 0:
      GOTO 7490
 7340 L1 = 3:
      GOTO 7490
 7490 RETURN
 7500 REM  OPENER REBID
 7503 IF OPB(H) # 7 THEN 7505:
      GOSUB 11000:
      IF S1 = 0 THEN 7930:
      GOSUB 14000:
```

```
           GOTO 7990
7505 IF OPB(H) < 10 THEN 7990
7507 IF (OPB(PH) MOD 100) / 10 > 1 THEN 7530
7508 IF OPB(PH) MOD 10 = 6 THEN 7900
7510 IF HCNT(H) > 15 THEN 7600
7520 IF OPB(H) = 15 THEN 7990
7530 FS = OPB(PH) MOD 10:
     IF SUCNT((H - 1) * 4 + 5 - FS) < 6 THEN 7540:
     S1 = FS:
     GOSUB 14000:
     GOTO 7990
7540 PS = OPB(H) MOD 10
7545 IF PS > 4 THEN 7560
7550 GOSUB 13000:
     IF S1 = 0 THEN 7560:
     GOSUB 14000:
     GOTO 7990
7560 GOSUB 12000:
     IF S1 = 0 THEN 7565:
     GOSUB 14000:
     IF L1 = 1 OR S1 < FS THEN 7990
7565 FS = OPB(PH) MOD 10:
     IF SUCNT((H - 1) * 4 + 5 - FS) < 5 THEN 7570:
     S1 = FS:
     GOSUB 14000:
     GOTO 7990
7570 S1 = 5:
     GOSUB 14000:
     IF L1 = 1 THEN 7990:
     L1 = 0:
     GOTO 7990
7600 IF OPB(PH) MOD 10 = 5 THEN 7900
7605 IF HCNT(H) > 18 THEN 7700
7610 MAX(H) = 18:
     FS = OPB(PH) MOD 10:
     IF SUCNT((H - 1) * 4 + 5 - FS) < 6 THEN 7615:
     S1 = FS:
     GOSUB 14000:
     L1 = L1 + 1:
     GOTO 7990
7615 PS = OPB(H) MOD 10:
     IF PS > 4 THEN 7630
7620 GOSUB 13000:
     IF S1 = 0 OR SUCNT((H - 1) * 4 + 5 - PS) < 4 THEN 7630:
     GOSUB 14000:
     L1 = L1 + 1:
```

```
          GOTO 7990
7630 GOSUB 12000:
     IF S1 = 0 THEN 7635:
     GOSUB 14000:
     L1 = L1 + 1:
     GOTO 7990
7635 FS = OPB(PH) MOD 10:
     IF SUCNT((H - 1) * 4 + 5 - FS) < 5 THEN 7640:
     S1 = FS:
     GOSUB 14000:
     L1 = L1 + 1:
     GOTO 7990
7640 S1 = 5:
     GOSUB 14000:
     IF L1 = 1 THEN L1 = 2:
     GOTO 7990
7700 MAX(H) = 21:
     FS = OPB(PH) MOD 10:
     IF SUCNT((H - 1) * 4 + 5 - FS) < 6 THEN 7705:
     S1 = FS:
     XL1 = GAME(S1):
     GOSUB 14000:
     IF L1 < XL1 THEN L1 = XL1:
     GOTO 7990
7705 PS = OPB(H) MOD 10:
     IF PS > 4 THEN 7720
7710 GOSUB 13000:
     IF S1 = 0 OR SUCNT((H - 1) * 4 + 5 - PS) < 4 THEN 7720:
     L1 = GAME(S1):
     GOTO 7990
7720 S1 = 5:
     GOSUB 14000:
     IF L1 < 3 THEN L1 = 3
7730 GOTO 7990
7900 PS = OPB(H) MOD 10:
     IF PS > 4 THEN 7920
7910 GOSUB 13000:
     IF S1 = 0 OR SUCNT((H - 1) * 4 + 5 - PS) < 4 THEN 7920:
     GOSUB 14000:
     GOTO 7990
7920 GOSUB 12000:
     IF S1 = 0 THEN 7930:
     GOSUB 14000:
     GOTO 7990
7930 S1 = 5:
     GOSUB 14000:
```

```basic
      GOTO 7990
 7990 IF L1 = 0 THEN 7995:
      IF S1 = 5 AND L1 > 3 THEN L1 = 0
 7992 IF OPB(H) = 35 AND OPB(PH) MOD 10 = 5 THEN L1 = 0
 7995 RETURN
 8000 REM  GENERAL BID
 8005 IF OPB(H) < 10 THEN 8490
 8010 POINTS = HCNT(H) + MAX(PH)
 8015 IF POINTS > 31 THEN 8030
 8020 IF OPB(H) = 51 OR OPB(H) = 52 OR OPB(H) = 43 OR OPB(H) =
 44 OR OPB(H) = 35 THEN 8490
 8025 IF LBID / 10 > 4 AND POINTS < 30 THEN 8490
 8030 BB = 0:
      FOR P = 1 TO 4:
      IF SUBID((H - 1) * 4 + 5 - P) > 0 AND SUBID((PH - 1) * 4
 + 5 - P) > 0 THEN BB = P:
      NEXT P
 8040 B2 = 0:
      FOR P = 1 TO 4:
      IF SUBID((PH - 1) * 4 + 5 - P) > 1 THEN B2 = P:
      NEXT P
 8060 PS = OPB(H) MOD 10
 8070 IF BB = 0 THEN 8090:
      GOSUB 16000:
      IF BWD # 1 THEN 8080:
      BLBID = BB:
      GOTO 8490
 8080 S1 = BB:
      GOSUB 14000:
      GOTO 8300
 8090 IF B2 = 0 THEN 8100:
      IF SUCNT((H - 1) * 4 + 5 - B2) < 2 THEN 8100:
      GOSUB 16000:
      IF BWD # 1 THEN 8095:
      BLBID = B2:
      GOTO 8490
 8095 S1 = B2:
      GOSUB 14000:
      GOTO 8300
 8100 IF PS = 5 THEN 8130
 8110 IF PS = BB AND PS = B2 THEN 8130:
      GOSUB 13000:
      IF S1 = 0 THEN 8130:
      BLBID = S1:
      GOSUB 16000:
      IF BWD # 1 THEN 8120:
```

71

```
     GOTO 8490
8120 GOSUB 14000:
     GOTO 8300
8130 OS = 0:
     FOR P = 1 TO 4:
     IF SUBID((PH - 1) * 4 + 5 - P) = 0 THEN 8140:
     PS = P:
     GOSUB 13000:
     IF S1 = 0 THEN 8140
8135 OS = S1
8140 NEXT P
8142 IF OS > 0 THEN 8150
8145 FOR P = 1 TO 4:
     IF SUCNT((H - 1) * 4 + 5 - P) < 6 THEN 8147:
     S1 = P:
     OS = S1
8147 NEXT P
8150 IF OS = 0 THEN 8200:
     GOSUB 16000:
     IF BWD # 1 THEN 8160:
     BLBID = OS:
     GOTO 8490
8160 S1 = OS:
     GOSUB 14000:
     GOTO 8300
8200 GOSUB 16000:
     IF BWD # 1 THEN 8250:
     BLBID = 5:
     GOTO 8490
8250 S1 = 5:
     GOSUB 14000
8300 IF L1 > 3 THEN 8320:
     IF POINTS > 25 AND S1 = 5 THEN 8490:
     IF POINTS > 20 AND S1 # 5 THEN 8490:
     L1 = 0:
     GOTO 8490
8320 IF L1 > 4 THEN 8340:
     IF POINTS > 25 THEN 8490:
     L1 = 0:
     GOTO 8490
8340 IF POINTS > 28 THEN 8345:
     L1 = 0:
     GOTO 8490
8345 IF POINTS > 32 THEN 8350:
     IF L1 > 5 THEN L1 = 0:
     GOTO 8490
```

72

```
8350 IF POINTS > 36 THEN 8360:
     IF L1 > 6 THEN L1 = 0:
     GOTO 8490
8360 IF L1 > 7 THEN L1 = 0:
     GOTO 8490
8490 RETURN
9000 REM  GET SOUTH BID
9020 VTAB 22:
     TAB 18:
     PRINT "?     "
9040 VTAB 22:
     TAB 18:
     INPUT SS$
9045 IF LEN(SS$) = 0 THEN SS$ = "PASS"
9050 IF LEN(SS$) > 1 THEN 9060:
     KIX = 0:
     GOTO 9100
9060 SS$ = SS$(1,2)
9070 KIX = 0:
     FOR IX = 1 TO 38
9080 IF SS$=BID$(2 * IX - 1,2 * IX) THEN KIX = IX
9090 NEXT IX
9100 IF KIX # 0 THEN 9105:
     FOR BUZ = 1 TO 20:
     SOUND = PEEK (-16336):
     NEXT BUZ:
     GOTO 9020
9105 IF BWD > 0 AND OPB(3) > 10 THEN BWD = BWD + 1:
     IF KIX = 23 THEN BWD = 1
9110 IF KIX # 1 THEN 9120:
     PCNT = PCNT + 1:
     GOSUB 9500:
     GOTO 9200
9120 IF KIX # 2 THEN 9125:
     IF R(H) # 1 THEN 9122:
     S1 = 106:
     L1 = 1:
     GOTO 9200
9122 S1 = 6:
     L1 = 1:
     GOSUB 10600:
     GOTO 9400
9125 IF KIX # 3 THEN 9140:
     IF DBL # 1 THEN 9130:
     S1 = 7:
     L1 = 1:
```

```
      GOSUB 10600:
      MAX(H) = 12:
      GOTO 9400
 9130 KIX = 0:
      GOTO 9100
 9140 L1 = (KIX - 4) / 5 + 1:
      S1 = (KIX - 3) MOD 5:
      IF S1 = 0 THEN S1 = 5
 9142 IF LBID MOD 100 < L1 * 10 + S1 THEN 9145:
      L1 = 0:
      KIX = 0:
      GOTO 9100
 9145 IF LBID = 0 THEN S1 = S1 + 100
 9150 REM
 9200 IF L1 = 0 THEN 9400
 9210 IF S1 = 106 THEN MAX(H) = 15
 9215 IF S1 = 7 THEN MAX(H) = 10
 9220 IF LBID = 0 THEN MAX(H) = 15 - 5 * (L1 = 3)
 9225 IF OPB(PH) # 0 THEN 9280
 9230 IF LBID = 0 AND L1 = 2 AND S1 MOD 10 # 5 THEN 9235:
      GOTO 9240
 9235 MAX(H) = 23:
      GOTO 9300
 9240 IF LBID # 0 THEN 9260:
      IF S1 MOD 10 # 5 THEN 9260:
      IF L1 = 1 THEN MAX(H) = 18:
      IF L1 = 2 THEN MAX(H) = 24:
      IF L1 > 2 THEN MAX(H) = 27
 9260 IF OPB(H) < 109 THEN 9267:
      IF L1 = 1 THEN MAX(H) = 9:
      IF S1 # OPB(H) MOD 10 THEN 9267:
      IF L1 = (OPB(H) MOD 100) / 10 + 1 THEN MAX(H) = 9
 9265 IF L1 > (OPB(H) MOD 100) / 10 + 1 THEN MAX(H) = 13:
      GOTO 9300
 9267 IF LBID = 0 THEN 9290
 9270 IF L1 = 1 THEN MAX = 9:
      IF L1 > 1 THEN MAX = 12:
      IF MAX(H) < MAX THEN MAX(H) = MAX
 9275 IF OPB(H) = 0 THEN 9290
 9280 IF S1 > LBID MOD 10 AND L1 > (LBID MOD 100) / 10 THEN
MAX(H) = 19:
      IF S1 < LBID MOD 10 AND L1 > (LBID MOD 100) / 10 + 1
THEN MAX(H) = 19
 9285 IF L1 = 3 THEN MAX = 21 - MAX(PH):
      IF L1 = 4 THEN MAX = 26 - MAX(PH):
      IF MAX > MAX(H) THEN MAX(H) = MAX
```

```
9290 REM
9300 GOSUB 10600
9400 RETURN
9500 REM  PASS
9505 OPB(PH) = 0
9510 IF H # 1 THEN 9520:
     VT = 16:
     HT = 18:
     GOTO 9600
9520 IF H # 2 THEN 9540:
     VT = 19:
     HT = 31:
     GOTO 9600
9540 IF H # 3 THEN 9560:
     VT = 22:
     HT = 18:
     GOTO 9600
9560 VT = 19:
     HT = 6:
     GOTO 9600
9600 VTAB VT:
     TAB HT:
     PRINT "     ":
     CALL -198:
     VTAB VT:
     TAB HT:
     PRINT "PASS":
     RETURN
10500 IF DEAL(I) > 39 THEN SURK((H - 1) * 4 + 1) = SURK((H -
1) * 4 + 1) + RANK
10510 IF DEAL(I) < 40 AND DEAL(I) > 26 THEN SURK((H - 1) * 4 +
2) = SURK((H - 1) * 4 + 2) + RANK
10520 IF DEAL(I) < 27 AND DEAL(I) > 13 THEN SURK((H - 1) * 4 +
3) = SURK((H - 1) * 4 + 3) + RANK
10530 IF DEAL(I) < 14 THEN SURK((H - 1) * 4 + 4) = SURK((H -
1) * 4 + 4) + RANK
10540 RETURN
10600 REM  DISPLAY BID
10605 IF S1 # 6 THEN 10610:
     OPB(PH) = 6:
     GOTO 10700
10610 IF S1 # 7 THEN 10620:
     OPB(PH) = 7:
     GOTO 10700
10620 IF S1 # 106 THEN 10640:
     OPB(PH) = 106:
```

```
      GOTO 10700
10640 LBID = 10 * L1 + S1:
      IF DCS(S1 MOD 10) = 0 THEN DCS(S1 MOD 10) = H
10660 OPB(PH) = LBID
10670 SM10 = S1 MOD 10
10680 IF SM10 < 5 AND BWD = 0 THEN SUBID((H - 1) * 4 + 5 -
SM10) = SUBID((H - 1) * 4 + 5 - SM10) + 1
10700 PCNT = 0
10710 IF S1 # 7 THEN 10720:
      IX = 5:
      DBL = 2:
      GOTO 10800
10720 IF S1 MOD 10 # 6 THEN 10730:
      IX = 3:
      DBL = 1:
      GOTO 10800
10730 S1 = S1 MOD 100:
      IX = ((L1 - 1) * 5 + S1) * 2 + 5
10750 DBL = 0
10800 IF H # 1 THEN 10820:
      VT = 16:
      HT = 18:
      GOTO 10900
10820 IF H # 2 THEN 10840:
      VT = 19:
      HT = 31:
      GOTO 10900
10840 IF H # 3 THEN 10860:
      VT = 22:
      HT = 18:
      GOTO 10900
10860 VT = 19:
      HT = 6
10900 VTAB VT:
      TAB HT:
      PRINT "    ":
      CALL -198:
      VTAB VT:
      TAB HT:
      PRINT BID$(IX,IX + 1):
      CALL -198:
      RETURN
11000 S1 = 0:
      TEMP = 0:
      FOR P = 1 TO 4
11010 BS = (H - 1) * 4 + P
```

```
11020 IF TAL(BS) <= TEMP OR TAL(BS) < 14 THEN 11040
11030 TEMP = TAL(BS):
      S1 = 5 - P
11040 NEXT P
11050 RETURN
12000 S1 = 0:
      TEMP = 0:
      FOR P = 1 TO 4
12010 BS = (H - 1) * 4 + P
12020 IF TAL(BS) <= TEMP OR TAL(BS) < 14 OR FS = 5 - P THEN
12040
12030 TEMP = TAL(BS):
      S1 = 5 - P
12040 NEXT P
12050 RETURN
13000 REM  CHECK SUPPORT
13010 S1 = 0:
      BS = (H - 1) * 4 + 5 - PS
13020 IF SUCNT(BS) > 3 THEN S1 = PS
13030 IF SUCNT(BS) = 3 AND SURK(BS) > 0 THEN S1 = PS
13040 RETURN
14000 REM  NEXT BID LEVEL
14010 L1 = (LBID MOD 100) / 10
14020 IF L1 * 10 + S1 > LBID MOD 100 THEN 14030:
      L1 = L1 + 1
14030 RETURN
15000 REM ---COMPUTER DOUBLE CHECK
15010 IF OPB(1) # LBID AND OPB(3) # LBID THEN 15900:
      IF DBL > 0 THEN 15900
15015 DCK = (LBID MOD 100) / 10
15020 IF DCK > 2 AND HCNT(H) + MAX(PH) > 22 THEN 15800
15040 IF DCK > 3 AND HCNT(H) + MAX(PH) > 16 THEN 15800
15060 IF DCK > 4 AND HCNT(H) + MAX(PH) > 11 THEN 15800
15080 IF DCK > 5 AND HCNT(H) + MAX(PH) > 8 THEN 15800
15100 GOTO 15900
15800 L1 = 1:
      S1 = 6
15900 RETURN
16000 REM  CHECK FOR SLAM
16010 IF LBID > 44 THEN 16100
16020 IF MAX(PH) + HCNT(H) < 32 + VUL THEN 16100
16040 L1 = 4:
      S1 = 5
16060 BWD = 1
16100 RETURN
17000 REM  BLACKWOOD CONVENTION
```

```
17020 IF BWD # 1 THEN 17200
17040 GOSUB 18000
17060 L1 = 5:
      S1 = ACNT + 1:
      IF S1 = 5 THEN S1 = 1
17080 GOTO 17800
17200 IF BWD # 2 THEN 17400
17210 GOSUB 18000
17220 IF LBID MOD 10 + ACNT - 1 = 4 THEN 17300
17230 IF LBID MOD 10 + ACNT - 1 = 0 THEN 17300
17240 L1 = 6:
      S1 = BLBID MOD 10:
      BWD = 0
17260 GOTO 17900
17300 L1 = 5:
      S1 = 5
17320 GOTO 17800
17400 IF BWD # 3 THEN 17600
17410 IF LBID MOD 10 # 5 THEN 17800
17415 IF LBID / 10 # 5 THEN 17800
17420 GOSUB 18500
17440 L1 = 6:
      S1 = KCNT + 1:
      IF S1 = 5 THEN S1 = 1
17460 GOTO 17800
17600 IF BWD # 4 THEN 17900
17620 GOSUB 18500
17640 IF LBID MOD 10 + KCNT - 1 = 4 THEN 17700
17650 IF LBID MOD 10 + KCNT - 1 = 0 THEN 17700
17660 L1 = 6:
      S1 = 5:
      BWD = 0:
      IF BLBID MOD 10 > LBID MOD 10 THEN S1 = BLBID MOD 10
17680 GOTO 17900
17700 L1 = 7:
      S1 = BLBID MOD 10:
      BWD = 0
17720 GOTO 17900
17800 BWD = BWD + 1
17900 RETURN
18000 REM  COUNT ACES
18005 ACNT = 0
18010 FOR P = (H - 1) * 13 + 1 TO (H - 1) * 13 + 13
18020 IF DEAL(P) MOD 13 = 0 THEN ACNT = ACNT + 1
18030 NEXT P
18040 RETURN
```

```
18500 REM  COUNT KINGS
18510 KCNT = 0
18520 FOR P = (H - 1) * 13 + 1 TO (H - 1) * 13 + 13
18530 IF DEAL(P) MOD 13 = 12 THEN KCNT = KCNT + 1
18540 NEXT P
18550 RETURN
```

TRIK 1.0 PLAY Listing

```
Name     : TRIK 1.0 PLAY
Length   : $3092 (12434)

   50 DIM SYM$(104),SDEAL(52)
   52 CALL -936
   53 DEC = 0
   55 SYM$ =
"2C3C4C5C6C7C8C9CTCJCQCKCAC2D3D4D5D6D7D8D9DTDJDQDKDAD2H3H4H5H6
H7H8H9HTHJHQHKHAH2S3S4S5S6S7S8S9STSJSQSKSAS"
   57 DIM PL$(10)
   58 DIM SPC$(30):
      SPC$ = "                              "
   59 DLR = Q:
      D$ = "<ctrl-D>":
      REM  CNTL D IN QUOTES
   60 FOR P = 1 TO 52:
      PLAY(P) = P:
      SDEAL(P) = DEAL(P):
      NEXT P
   62 IF OPB(2) = 6 OR OPB(4) = 6 THEN 67:
      IF OPB(2) = 106 OR OPB(4) = 106 THEN 67
   63 IF OPB(1) = 7 OR OPB(3) = 7 THEN 67
   65 IF OPB(1) # LBID AND OPB(3) # LBID THEN 32000
   67 IF DCS(LBID MOD 10) # 1 THEN 70:
      GOSUB 32200:
      FOR DELAY = 1 TO 500:
      NEXT DELAY:
      CALL -936
   70 CALL -384:
      TAB 18:
      PRINT "DUMMY":
      CALL -380
   80 POKE 32,8:
      PRINT
   90 ST = 1:
      GOSUB 2000
  100 VTAB 16:
      CALL -384:
      TAB 10:
      PRINT "SOUTH":
      CALL -380:
      PRINT
```

```
110 ST = 27:
    GOSUB 2000
120 POKE 32,0
130 WE = 0:
    THEY = 0
140 VTAB 23:
    PRINT "BID: ";CTR$;" ";XX$;:
    IF VUL = 0 THEN PRINT " N/V";:
    IF VUL = 1 THEN PRINT " VUL";
142 TAB 19:
    PRINT "TRICKS: WE-";WE;"  THEY-";THEY
145 VTAB 22:
    PRINT "--------------------------------------"
150 VTAB 11:
    CALL -384:
    PRINT "WEST"
160 VTAB 11:
    TAB 36:
    PRINT "EAST":
    CALL -380
165 FOR I = 1 TO 16:
    OUT(I) = 0:
    SUIT(I) = SUCNT(I):
    NEXT I
170 Q = 4
180 TRK = 13
190 T = LBID MOD 10:
    TRH = 52 * (T = 4) + 39 * (T = 3) + 26 * (T = 2) + 13 *
(T = 1):
    TRL = 40 * (T = 4) + 27 * (T = 3) + 14 * (T = 2) + 1 *
(T = 1)
200 REM  PLAY A TRICK
210 LEDL = 0:
    LEDH = 0:
    WCARD = 0
215 TRX = 0
217 CALL -198:
    CALL -198
220 FOR J = Q TO Q + 3
240 H = J:
    IF H > 4 THEN H = J - 4
260 IF H = 1 THEN GOSUB 3000
280 IF H = 2 THEN GOSUB 8000
300 IF H = 3 THEN GOSUB 4000
320 IF H = 4 THEN GOSUB 5000
340 NEXT J
```

```
400 Q = WINS
405 IF Q = 1 OR Q = 3 THEN WE = WE + 1:
    IF Q = 2 OR Q = 4 THEN THEY = THEY + 1
407 VTAB 23:
    TAB 30:
    PRINT WE:
    VTAB 23:
    TAB 38:
    PRINT THEY
410 IF H = 1 OR H = 3 THEN 420:
    FOR DELAY = 1 TO 350:
    NEXT DELAY
420 TRK = TRK - 1:
    IF TRK = 0 THEN 500
430 VTAB 11:
    TAB 10:
    PRINT "    ":
    VTAB 11:
    TAB 29:
    PRINT "    "
440 VTAB 8:
    TAB 20:
    PRINT "     ":
    VTAB 14:
    TAB 20:
    PRINT "     "
460 GOTO 200
500 POKE 1338,72:
    POKE 1339,73:
    POKE 1340,84:
    POKE 1465,82:
    POKE 1466,69:
    POKE 1467,84:
    POKE 1468,85:
    POKE 1469,82:
    POKE 1470,78
520 X = PEEK (-16384):
    IF X <= 127 THEN 520:
    POKE -16368,0:
    IF X # 141 THEN 520
540 CALL -936
560 OVTK = WE - 6 - ((LBID MOD 100) / 10)
580 VTAB 3:
    PRINT "CONTRACT: ";CTR$;" ";XX$;
590 IF VUL = 0 THEN PRINT " NOT VULNERABLE":
    IF VUL = 1 THEN PRINT " VULNERABLE"
```

```
600 VTAB 5:
    IF OVTK >= 0 THEN PRINT "YOU MADE IT! (";OVTK;"
OVERTRICKS)"
620 IF OVTK < 0 THEN PRINT "YOU WERE SET ";ABS(OVTK);"
TRICKS!"
640 VTAB 10:
    TAB 5:
    PRINT "1 -- DISPLAY THE HANDS"
660 TAB 5:
    PRINT "2 -- SAVE THIS HAND"
680 TAB 5:
    PRINT "3 -- REPLAY THIS CONTRACT"
700 TAB 5:
    PRINT "4 -- DEAL A NEW HAND"
720 TAB 5:
    PRINT "5 -- END"
740 VTAB 18:
    TAB 20:
    PRINT "ENTER YOUR CHOICE."
750 GOSUB 25000
760 X = PEEK (-16384):
    IF X <= 127 THEN 760:
    POKE -16368,0:
    IF X < 177 OR X > 181 THEN 760
780 IF X = 177 THEN 800
782 IF X = 178 THEN 820
784 IF X = 179 THEN 850
786 IF X = 180 THEN 900
788 IF X = 181 THEN 1000
800 FOR I = 1 TO 52:
    DEAL(I) = SDEAL(I):
    NEXT I
810 GOSUB 20000:
    GOTO 540
820 CALL -936:
    PRINT "ENTER HAND NUMBER (1-99):":
    INPUT HN
825 PRINT D$;"OPEN HAND ";HN
827 PRINT D$;"WRITE HAND ";HN
830 FOR I = 1 TO 52:
    PRINT SDEAL(I):
    NEXT I:
    PRINT DLR:
    PRINT VUL
835 PRINT D$;"CLOSE HAND ";HN
840 PRINT:
```

```
      PRINT "HAND ";HN;" SAVED":
      VTAB 20:
      INPUT "HIT RETURN ",A$
 845 GOTO 540
 850 FOR I = 1 TO 52:
      DEAL(I) = SDEAL(I):
      NEXT I
 860 CALL -936:
      GOTO 60
 900 PRINT D$;"RUN TRIK 1.0 BID"
1000 CALL -936:
      END
1200 REM    COUNT HIGHER CARDS IN SUIT
1220 HISU = 0
1240 FOR I = SSL TO SSH
1260 IF PLAY(I) > DEAL(P) THEN HISU = HISU + 1
1280 NEXT I
1290 IF TRX = 1 AND SSL # TRL THEN 1340
1295 IF HISU = 0 AND LEDL = 0 THEN WC = P
1300 IF HISU = 0 AND LEDL = SSL AND WCARD < DEAL(P) THEN WC =
P
1320 IF HISU = 2 AND LEDL = SSL AND WCARD < DEAL(P) THEN FC =
P
1340 RETURN
1500 REM    SET SSL AND SSH
1520 ACD = DEAL(P)
1540 SSL = ((ACD - 1) / 13) * 13 + 1
1560 SSH = ((ACD - 1) / 13) * 13 + 13
1580 RETURN
2000 PRINT "SPADES:   ";
2010 CALL -384:
      FOR P = ST TO ST + 12
2015 IF DEAL(P) <= 39 THEN 2030
2020 IF RK$(DEAL(P),DEAL(P))#"T" THEN 2025:
      PRINT "10 ";:
      GOTO 2030
2025 PRINT RK$(DEAL(P),DEAL(P));" ";
2030 NEXT P:
      CALL -380:
      PRINT ""
2040 PRINT "HEARTS:   ";
2050 CALL -384:
      FOR P = ST TO ST + 12
2055 IF DEAL(P) >= 40 OR DEAL(P) <= 26 THEN 2070
2060 IF RK$(DEAL(P),DEAL(P))#"T" THEN 2065:
      PRINT "10 ";:
```

```
      GOTO 2070
2065 PRINT RK$(DEAL(P),DEAL(P));" ";
2070 NEXT P:
      CALL -380:
      PRINT ""
2080 PRINT "DIAMONDS:";
2090 CALL -384:
      FOR P = ST TO ST + 12
2095 IF DEAL(P) >= 27 OR DEAL(P) <= 13 THEN 2110
2100 IF RK$(DEAL(P),DEAL(P))#"T" THEN 2105:
      PRINT "10 ";:
      GOTO 2110
2105 PRINT RK$(DEAL(P),DEAL(P));" ";
2110 NEXT P:
      CALL -380:
      PRINT ""
2120 PRINT "CLUBS:    ";
2130 CALL -384:
      FOR P = ST TO ST + 12
2132 IF DEAL(P) = 0 THEN 2150
2135 IF DEAL(P) >= 14 THEN 2150
2140 IF RK$(DEAL(P),DEAL(P))#"T" THEN 2145:
      PRINT "10 ";:
      GOTO 2150
2145 PRINT RK$(DEAL(P),DEAL(P));" ";
2150 NEXT P:
      CALL -380:
      PRINT ""
2160 RETURN
3000 REM  NORTH PLAY
3020 VTAB 8:
      TAB 20
3030 PRINT "?       "
3040 VTAB 8:
      TAB 20:
      INPUT PL$
3045 IF PL$#"LD" THEN 3050:
      TRK = 1:
      WE = 13 - THEY:
      POP :
      FOR J = 1 TO 1:
      NEXT J:
      GOTO 420
3050 IF LEN(PL$) # 2 THEN 3200
3055 MTCH = 0
3060 GOSUB 3500:
```

```
         IF MTCH = 0 THEN 3200
3070 GOSUB 4500
3080 VTAB 2:
     POKE 32,8:
     PRINT:
     PRINT SPC$:
     PRINT SPC$:
     PRINT SPC$:
     PRINT SPC$:
     VTAB 3
3090 ST = 1:
     GOSUB 2000:
     POKE 32,0
3095 CALL -198
3100 RETURN
3200 FOR BUZ = 1 TO 50:
     S = PEEK (-16336):
     NEXT BUZ
3210 GOTO 3020
3500 REM  CHECK PLAY FOR LEGAL
3510 IF MTCH # 0 THEN 3590
3520 MTCH = 0:
     FOR M = 1 TO 52
3540 M2 = (M - 1) * 2 + 1:
     IF PL$#SYM$(M2,M2 + 1) THEN 3560:
     MTCH = M:
     M = 52
3560 NEXT M
3580 IF MTCH = 0 THEN 3900
3590 IF LEDL = 0 THEN 3620
3600 IF MTCH > LEDH OR MTCH < LEDL THEN 3800
3620 IF H MOD 2 = 0 THEN 3900:
     GOT = 0:
     FOR M = (H - 1) * 13 + 1 TO (H - 1) * 13 + 13
3630 IF MTCH # DEAL(M) THEN 3650
3640 GOT = 1
3650 NEXT M
3660 IF GOT = 1 THEN 3900
3670 MTCH = 0:
     GOTO 3900
3800 IF SUIT((H - 1) * 4 + 4 - (LEDL / 13)) = 0 THEN 3620
3840 MTCH = 0:
     GOTO 3900
3900 RETURN
4000 REM  SOUTH PLAY
4020 VTAB 14:
```

```
       TAB 20
 4030 PRINT "?        "
 4040 VTAB 14:
       TAB 20:
       INPUT PL$
 4045 IF PL$#"LD" THEN 4050:
       TRK = 1:
       WE = 13 - THEY:
       POP :
       FOR J = 1 TO 1:
       NEXT J:
       GOTO 420
 4050 IF LEN(PL$) # 2 THEN 4200
 4055 MTCH = 0
 4060 GOSUB 3500:
       IF MTCH = 0 THEN 4200
 4070 GOSUB 4500
 4080 VTAB 17:
       POKE 32,8:
       PRINT:
       PRINT SPC$:
       PRINT SPC$:
       PRINT SPC$:
       PRINT SPC$:
       VTAB 18
 4090 ST = 27:
       GOSUB 2000:
       POKE 32,0
 4095 CALL -198
 4100 RETURN
 4200 FOR BUZ = 1 TO 50:
       S = PEEK (-16336):
       NEXT BUZ
 4210 GOTO 4020
 4500 REM   RECORD PLAY
 4510 X = (H - 1) * 4 + 4 - ((MTCH - 1) / 13):
       SUIT(X) = SUIT(X) - 1
 4520 IF LEDL # 0 THEN 4540
 4525 WCARD = MTCH:
       WINS = H
 4530 LEDH = 52 * (MTCH > 39) + 39 * (MTCH < 40 AND MTCH > 26)
+ 26 * (MTCH < 27 AND MTCH > 13) + 13 * (MTCH < 14)
 4535 LEDL = 40 * (MTCH > 39) + 27 * (MTCH < 40 AND MTCH > 26)
+ 14 * (MTCH < 27 AND MTCH > 13) + 1 * (MTCH < 14)
 4537 IF H # 2 THEN 4538:
       DEAL(BS + 13) = 0:
```

```
      GOTO 4547
4538 IF H # 4 THEN 4540:
     DEAL(BS + 39) = 0:
     GOTO 4547
4540 FOR M = 1 TO 52:
     IF DEAL(M) # MTCH THEN 4545:
     DEAL(M) = 0:
     M = 52
4545 NEXT M
4547 IF H = 1 AND SUIT(X) < 1 THEN OUT(X) = 1:
     IF LEDL <= MTCH AND LEDH >= MTCH THEN 4550:
     OUT((H - 1) * 4 + 4 - (LEDL / 13)) = 1
4550 PLAY(MTCH) = 0
4555 IF WCARD = MTCH THEN 4900
4560 IF WCARD > LEDH OR WCARD < LEDL THEN 4700
4580 IF MTCH > LEDH OR MTCH < LEDL THEN 4600
4590 IF MTCH < WCARD THEN 4900:
     WCARD = MTCH:
     WINS = H:
     GOTO 4900
4600 IF MTCH > TRH OR MTCH < TRL THEN 4900:
     WCARD = MTCH:
     WINS = H:
     TRX = 1:
     GOTO 4900
4700 IF MTCH > TRH OR MTCH < TRL THEN 4900:
     IF WCARD > MTCH THEN 4900:
     WCARD = MTCH:
     WINS = H:
     GOTO 4900
4900 RETURN
5000 REM  WEST PLAY
5010 WC = 0:
     FC = 0
5020 VTAB 11:
     TAB 10
5030 SSL = LEDL:
     SSH = LEDH:
     GOSUB 12000:
     GOSUB 13000:
     GOSUB 12500
5040 FOR P = 40 TO 52
5060 IF DEAL(P) = 0 THEN 6900
5065 IF LEDL = 0 THEN 5090
5070 MTCH = DEAL(P)
5080 GOSUB 3500:
```

89

```
      IF MTCH = 0 THEN 6900
 5090 GOSUB 1500
 5092 GOSUB 1200
 5095 VAL(P - 39) = HISU
 5100 IF TRL = 0 THEN 5104
 5102 IF DEAL(P) < TRL OR DEAL(P) > TRH THEN 5104:
      VAL(P - 39) = VAL(P - 39) - 10
 5104 IF LEDL # 0 THEN 5125:
      DM13 = (DEAL(P) - 1) / 13
 5106 IF SUBID(8 - DM13) > 0 THEN VAL(P - 39) = VAL(P - 39) +
30 - HISU * 2 * (TRK < 10)
 5108 IF SUBID(4 - DM13) = 0 AND SUBID(12 - DM13) = 0 THEN
VAL(P - 39) = VAL(P - 39) + 10 + SUIT(16 - DM13)
 5109 IF TRL = 0 THEN 5125:
      SC = 0:
      TC = 0:
      FOR I = 1 TO 4:
      SC = SC + SUIT(4 * I - DM13):
      TC = TC + SUIT(4 * I - TRL / 13):
      NEXT I
 5110 IF SC - SUIT(4 - DM13) - SUIT(16 - DM13) < 3 AND TC -
SUIT(4 - TRL / 13) - SUIT(16 - TRL / 13) > 0 AND OUT(8 - DM13)
= 0 THEN VAL(P - 39) = VAL(P - 39) + 25
 5114 IF SUIT(4 - DM13) = 0 AND SUIT(4 - TRL / 13) > 0 THEN
VAL(P - 39) = VAL(P - 39) - 100
 5116 IF OUT(12 - DM13) = 1 AND TC - SUIT(4 - TRL / 13) -
SUIT(16 - TRL / 13) > 0 THEN VAL(P - 39) = VAL(P - 39) - 20
 5118 IF OUT(8 - DM13) = 1 AND TC - SUIT(4 - TRL / 13) -
SUIT(16 - TRL / 13) > 0 THEN VAL(P - 39) = VAL(P - 39) + 50 *
(OUT(4 - DM13) = 0 AND OUT(12 - DM13) = 0)
 5119 IF TRL = 0 THEN 5125
 5120 IF TRK = 13 AND SUIT(16 - DM13) < 2 THEN VAL(P - 39) =
VAL(P - 39) + 10 * (DEAL(P) > TRH OR DEAL(P) < TRL)
 5122 IF TRK = 13 AND SUIT(16 - DM13) < 3 THEN VAL(P - 39) =
VAL(P - 39) + 5 * (DEAL(P) > TRH OR DEAL(P) < TRL)
 5125 IF WINS = 2 THEN 5200
 5130 IF TRX = 1 THEN 6000
 5140 IF WC = P THEN VAL(P - 39) = VAL(P - 39) + 50 * (LEDL #
0 OR TRK < 10 OR TRL # 0) - 40 * (DEAL(P) <= TRH AND DEAL(P)
>= TRL)
 5180 IF DEAL(P) < TRL OR DEAL(P) > TRH THEN 5200
 5185 IF LEDL = 0 THEN 5200
 5190 VAL(P - 39) = VAL(P - 39) + 50
 5200 IF P # LCD THEN 5230
 5220 IF Q = 3 THEN VAL(P - 39) = VAL(P - 39) + 30 + TRK
 5230 IF WINS = 2 THEN 5275
```

```
5240 IF P # CCD THEN 5275
5270 IF Q = 1 THEN VAL(P - 39) = VAL(P - 39) + 100
5275 IF Q = 3 THEN 5500
5280 IF Q # 2 THEN 7000
5300 IF WINS = 2 AND WCARD > DUM1 THEN 7000
5320 IF DEAL(P) > LEDH OR DEAL(P) < LEDL THEN 7000
5340 IF DEAL(P) > DUM1 THEN VAL(P - 39) = VAL(P - 39) + 65 *
(WC # P) * (WCARD < DEAL(P))
5350 IF WINS = 2 AND WCARD > DUM2 THEN 7000
5360 IF DEAL(P) > DUM2 THEN VAL(P - 39) = VAL(P - 39) + 20 *
(WCARD < DEAL(P))
5380 GOTO 7000
5500 IF DEAL(P) > LEDH OR DEAL(P) < LEDL THEN 7000
5510 IF TRL = 0 THEN 5520:
     IF SUIT(4 - TRL / 13) > 0 AND SUIT(4 - LEDL / 13) = 0
THEN 7000
5520 IF DEAL(P) > DUM1 AND DEAL(P) > WCARD THEN VAL(P - 39) =
VAL(P - 39) + 100
5540 GOTO 7000
6000 IF SSL # TRL THEN 7000
6020 CCD = 0:
     GOSUB 12000:
     IF CCD = P THEN 6060
6040 VAL(P - 39) = VAL(P - 39) - 50:
     GOTO 7000
6060 VAL(P - 39) = VAL(P - 39) + 70:
     GOTO 7000
6900 VAL(P - 39) = -200
7000 NEXT P
7010 BS = 0:
     TEMP = -100
7100 FOR P = 1 TO 13
7120 IF VAL(P) <= TEMP THEN 7500
7140 BS = P:
     TEMP = VAL(P)
7500 NEXT P
7520 MTCH = DEAL(39 + BS)
7880 GOSUB 4500:
     PRINT SYM$(MTCH * 2 - 1,MTCH * 2)
7890 IF TRK = 13 THEN SULD = (DEAL(P) - 1) / 13
7895 CALL -198
7900 RETURN
8000 REM  EAST PLAY
8010 WC = 0:
     FC = 0
8020 VTAB 11:
```

```
      TAB 29
 8030 SSL = LEDL:
      SSH = LEDH:
      GOSUB 12000:
      GOSUB 13000:
      GOSUB 12500
 8040 FOR P = 14 TO 26
 8060 IF DEAL(P) = 0 THEN 9900
 8065 IF LEDL = 0 THEN 8090
 8070 MTCH = DEAL(P)
 8080 GOSUB 3500:
      IF MTCH = 0 THEN 9900
 8090 GOSUB 1500
 8092 GOSUB 1200
 8095 VAL(P - 13) = HISU
 8100 IF TRL = 0 THEN 8104
 8102 IF DEAL(P) < TRL OR DEAL(P) > TRH THEN 8104:
      VAL(P - 13) = VAL(P - 13) - 10
 8104 DM13 = (DEAL(P) - 1) / 13:
      IF LEDL # 0 THEN 8125
 8105 IF SULD = DM13 THEN VAL(P - 13) = VAL(P - 13) + 10
 8106 IF SUBID(16 - DM13) > 0 THEN VAL(P - 13) = VAL(P - 13) +
30 - HISU * 2 * (TRK < 10)
 8108 IF SUBID(4 - DM13) = 0 AND SUBID(12 - DM13) = 0 THEN
VAL(P - 13) = VAL(P - 13) + 10 + SUIT(8 - DM13)
 8109 IF TRL = 0 THEN 8125:
      SC = 0:
      TC = 0:
      FOR I = 1 TO 4:
      SC = SC + SUIT(4 * I - DM13):
      TC = TC + SUIT(4 * I - TRL / 13):
      NEXT I
 8110 IF SC - SUIT(4 - DM13) - SUIT(8 - DM13) < 3 AND TC -
SUIT(4 - TRL / 13) - SUIT(8 - TRL / 13) > 0 AND OUT(16 - DM13)
= 0 THEN VAL(P - 13) = VAL(P - 13) + 25
 8114 IF SUIT(4 - DM13) = 0 AND SUIT(4 - TRL / 13) > 0 THEN
VAL(P - 13) = VAL(P - 13) - 100
 8116 IF OUT(12 - DM13) = 1 AND TC - SUIT(4 - TRL / 13) -
SUIT(8 - TRL / 13) > 0 THEN VAL(P - 13) = VAL(P - 13) - 20
 8118 IF OUT(16 - DM13) = 1 AND TC - SUIT(4 - TRL / 13) -
SUIT(8 - TRL / 13) > 0 THEN VAL(P - 13) = VAL(P - 13) + 50 *
(OUT(4 - DM13) = 0 AND OUT(12 - DM13) = 0)
 8125 IF WINS = 4 AND Q = 3 THEN 8200
 8130 IF TRX = 1 THEN 9000
 8135 IF WINS = 4 AND DEAL(P) = WCARD + 1 THEN 8200
```

```
 8140 IF WC = P THEN VAL(P - 13) = VAL(P - 13) + 50 * (LEDL #
0 OR TRK < 10 OR TRL # 0) - 40 * (DEAL(P) <= TRH AND DEAL(P)
>= TRL)
 8160 IF FC = P AND WC # 0 AND DUM1 > DEAL(P) THEN VAL(P - 13)
= VAL(P - 13) + 100
 8170 IF WINS = 4 THEN 8200
 8180 IF DEAL(P) < TRL OR DEAL(P) > TRH THEN 8200
 8185 IF LEDL = 0 THEN 8200
 8190 VAL(P - 13) = VAL(P - 13) + 50
 8200 IF P # LCD THEN 8230
 8220 IF Q = 1 THEN VAL(P - 13) = VAL(P - 13) + 30 + TRK
 8230 IF WINS = 4 THEN 8280
 8240 IF P # CCD THEN 8280
 8270 IF Q = 3 THEN VAL(P - 13) = VAL(P - 13) + 100
 8280 IF Q # 4 AND OUT(16 - DM13) # 1 THEN 10000
 8300 IF WINS = 4 AND (WCARD MOD 13 = 0 OR WCARD MOD 13 > 6)
THEN 10000
 8320 IF DEAL(P) > LEDH OR DEAL(P) < LEDL THEN 10000
 8330 IF DEAL(P) < WCARD THEN 10000
 8340 IF DEAL(P) MOD 13 = 0 OR DEAL(P) MOD 13 > 8 THEN VAL(P -
13) = VAL(P - 13) + 50 + DEAL(P) * (Q = 4)
 8360 GOTO 10000
 9000 IF SSL # TRL THEN 10000
 9020 CCD = 0:
      GOSUB 12000:
      IF CCD # 0 THEN 9060
 9040 VAL(P - 13) = VAL(P - 13) - 50:
      GOTO 10000
 9060 VAL(P - 13) = VAL(P - 13) + 70:
      GOTO 10000
 9900 VAL(P - 13) = -200
10000 NEXT P
10010 BS = 0:
      TEMP = -100
10100 FOR P = 1 TO 13
10120 IF VAL(P) <= TEMP THEN 10500
10140 BS = P:
      TEMP = VAL(P)
10500 NEXT P
10520 MTCH = DEAL(13 + BS)
10880 GOSUB 4500:
      PRINT SYM$(MTCH * 2 - 1,MTCH * 2)
10890 CALL -198
10900 RETURN
12000 REM  COVER
12010 CCD = 0:
```

```
      TEMP = 0
12020 FOR I = (H - 1) * 13 + 1 TO (H - 1) * 13 + 13
12030 IF DEAL(I) > SSH OR DEAL(I) < SSL THEN 12090
12035 IF TRX = 1 AND SSL # TRL THEN 12090
12040 IF DEAL(I) < WCARD THEN 12090
12050 IF DEAL(I) > TEMP AND TEMP # 0 THEN 12090
12060 TEMP = DEAL(I):
      CCD = I
12090 NEXT I:
      RETURN
12500 REM DUMMY HIGH
12520 DUM1 = 0:
      DUM2 = 0
12540 FOR I = 1 TO 13
12560 IF DEAL(I) < SSL OR DEAL(I) > SSH THEN 12600
12580 IF DEAL(I) < DUM1 THEN 12597
12590 TEMP = DUM1:
      DUM1 = DEAL(I)
12595 IF TEMP > DUM2 THEN DUM2 = TEMP:
      GOTO 12600
12597 IF DEAL(I) > DUM2 THEN DUM2 = DEAL(I)
12600 NEXT I
12700 RETURN
13000 REM   LOW
13010 LCD = 0:
      TEMP = 0
13020 FOR I = (H - 1) * 13 + 1 TO (H - 1) * 13 + 13
13030 IF DEAL(I) > SSH OR DEAL(I) < SSL THEN 13090
13040 IF DEAL(I) > TEMP AND TEMP # 0 THEN 13090
13050 TEMP = DEAL(I):
      LCD = I
13090 NEXT I:
      RETURN
20000 CALL -936
20020 POKE 32,6
20040 PRINT
20060 ST = 1:
      GOSUB 2000
20080 POKE 32,8:
      PRINT
20100 ST = 14:
      GOSUB 2000
20120 POKE 32,6:
      PRINT
20140 ST = 27:
      GOSUB 2000
```

```
20160 POKE 32,8:
      PRINT
20180 ST = 40:
      GOSUB 2000
20200 CALL -384
20220 POKE 32,0
20240 VTAB 3:
      PRINT "DUMMY"
20260 VTAB 8:
      PRINT "EAST"
20280 VTAB 13:
      PRINT "SOUTH"
20300 VTAB 18:
      PRINT "WEST"
20320 CALL -380
20340 VTAB 23:
      INPUT "HIT RETURN ",A$
20360 RETURN
25000 REM  CHICAGO SCORING
25020 IF OVTK >= 0 THEN 25200
25040 IF VUL = 1 THEN 25100
25050 IF DBL > 0 THEN 25080
25060 CHI = 50 * OVTK:
      GOTO 25400
25080 CHI = -DBL * (100 - 200 * (OVTK + 1)):
      GOTO 25400
25100 IF DBL > 0 THEN 25150
25110 CHI = 100 * OVTK:
      GOTO 25400
25150 CHI = -DBL * (200 - 300 * (OVTK + 1)):
      GOTO 25400
25200 LTV = LBID MOD 10:
      TV = 30 * (LTV > 2) + 20 * (LTV < 3)
25230 UNL = (2^DBL) * (((LBID MOD 100) / 10) * TV + 10 * (LTV
= 5))
25235 CHI = UNL + TV * OVTK * (DBL = 0) + DBL * (VUL + 1) *
100 * OVTK
25240 CHI = CHI + 50 * (DBL > 0)
25250 CHI = CHI + (UNL >= 100) * (300 + 200 * VUL)
25260 CHI = CHI + 50 * (UNL < 100)
25270 CHI = CHI + ((LBID MOD 100) / 10 = 6) * (500 + 250 *
VUL) + ((LBID MOD 100) / 10 = 7) * (1000 + 500 * VUL)
25400 VTAB 5:
      TAB 30:
      PRINT "SCORE"
25420 VTAB 6:
```

```
      TAB 30:
      CALL -384:
      PRINT "       "
25430 ACHI = ABS(CHI):
      TBA = 1 + (ACHI > 9) + (ACHI > 99) + (ACHI > 999) + (CHI
< 0)
25440 VTAB 6:
      TAB (35 - TBA):
      PRINT CHI:
      CALL -380
25460 RETURN
32000 VTAB 5:
      TAB 5:
      PRINT "ONLY EAST-WEST DEFENSE":
      PRINT:
      TAB 5:
      PRINT "IS CURRENTLY AVAILABLE."
32010 VTAB 10:
      TAB 5:
      PRINT "WOULD YOU LIKE TO PLAY WEST'S CARDS?":
      TAB 5:
      INPUT "(Y/N) ",A$
32020 IF A$="N" THEN PRINT D$;"RUN TRIK 1.0 BID"
32030 IF A$#"Y" THEN 32010
32035 CALL -936:
      PRINT "SWITCHING HANDS"
32040 FOR I = 1 TO 13
32050 TEMP = DEAL(I):
      DEAL(I) = DEAL(39 + I):
      DEAL(39 + I) = TEMP:
      TEMP = DEAL(13 + I):
      DEAL(13 + I) = DEAL(26 + I):
      DEAL(26 + I) = TEMP
32060 TEMP = DEAL(I):
      DEAL(I) = DEAL(26 + I):
      DEAL(26 + I) = TEMP
32070 NEXT I
32080 FOR I = 1 TO 4
32090 TEMP = SUCNT(I):
      SUCNT(I) = SUCNT(12 + I):
      SUCNT(12 + I) = TEMP:
      TEMP = SUCNT(4 + I):
      SUCNT(4 + I) = SUCNT(8 + I):
      SUCNT(8 + I) = TEMP
32100 TEMP = SUBID(I):
      SUBID(I) = SUBID(12 + I):
```

```
      SUBID(12 + I) = TEMP:
      TEMP = SUBID(4 + I):
      SUBID(4 + I) = SUBID(8 + I):
      SUBID(8 + I) = TEMP
32110 TEMP = SUCNT(I):
      SUCNT(I) = SUCNT(8 + I):
      SUCNT(8 + I) = TEMP:
      TEMP = SUBID(I):
      SUBID(I) = SUBID(8 + I):
      SUBID(8 + I) = TEMP
32120 NEXT I
32130 TEMP = OPB(1):
      OPB(1) = OPB(4):
      OPB(4) = TEMP:
      TEMP = OPB(2):
      OPB(2) = OPB(3):
      OPB(3) = TEMP
32140 TEMP = OPB(1):
      OPB(1) = OPB(3):
      OPB(3) = TEMP
32150 CALL -936:
      GOTO 60
32200 CALL -936:
      VTAB 12:
      PRINT "NORTH WAS DECLARER:":
      PRINT:
      PRINT "SWITCHING HANDS":
      FOR I = 1 TO 13
32220 TEMP = DEAL(I):
      DEAL(I) = DEAL(26 + I):
      DEAL(26 + I) = TEMP:
      TEMP = DEAL(13 + I):
      DEAL(13 + I) = DEAL(39 + I):
      DEAL(39 + I) = TEMP
32240 NEXT I
32260 FOR I = 1 TO 4
32280 TEMP = SUCNT(I):
      SUCNT(I) = SUCNT(8 + I):
      SUCNT(8 + I) = TEMP:
      TEMP = SUCNT(4 + I):
      SUCNT(4 + I) = SUCNT(12 + I):
      SUCNT(12 + I) = TEMP
32300 TEMP = SUBID(I):
      SUBID(I) = SUBID(8 + I):
      SUBID(8 + I) = TEMP:
      TEMP = SUBID(4 + I):
```

```
       SUBID(4 + I) = SUBID(12 + I):
       SUBID(12 + I) = TEMP
32320 NEXT I
32340 TEMP = OPB(1):
      OPB(1) = OPB(3):
      OPB(3) = TEMP:
      TEMP = OPB(2):
      OPB(2) = OPB(4):
      OPB(4) = TEMP
32360 DEC = 1
32380 RETURN
```

Build-A-Hand Listing

```
Name    : BUILD-A-HAND
Length  : $09CC (2508)

  10 POKE -16298,0:
     TEXT:
     CALL -936
  50 DIM DEAL(52), SYM$(104)
  55 SYM$ =
"2C3C4C5C6C7C8C9CTCJCQCKCAC2D3D4D5D6D7D8D9DTDJDQDKDAD2H3H4H5H6
H7H8H9HTHJHQHKHAH2S3S4S5S6S7S8S9STSJSQSKSAS"
  60 DIM A$(10)
  70 DIM CHECK(52)
 100 FOR I = 1 TO 52:
     CHECK(I) = 0:
     NEXT I
1000 CALL -936:
     VTAB 10:
     TAB 5:
     PRINT "BUILD YOUR OWN BRIDGE HANDS"
1020 VTAB 22:
     TAB 9:
     PRINT "*** HIT RETURN ***"
1040 X = PEEK (-16384):
     IF X <= 127 THEN 1040:
     POKE -16368,0:
     IF X # 141 THEN 1040
1060 CALL -936:
     CALL -198:
     CALL -198
1080 PRINT:
     PRINT "ENTER NORTH CARDS:"
1090 PRINT
1100 FOR I = 1 TO 13
1105 INPUT A$
1110 OK = 0
1120 FOR M = 1 TO 52:
     IF A$#SYM$(2 * M - 1,2 * M) THEN 1160
1140 OK = M:
     M = 52
1160 NEXT M
1180 IF OK > 0 THEN 1200:
     TAB 5:
```

```
      PRINT "*** INVALID CARD - REENTER ***":
      CALL -198:
      GOTO 1105
1200 IF CHECK(OK) = 0 THEN 1240
1220 TAB 5:
      PRINT "*** CARD ALREADY USED ***":
      CALL -198:
      GOTO 1105
1240 CHECK(OK) = 1:
      DEAL(I) = OK
1300 NEXT I
1360 CALL -936:
      CALL -198:
      CALL -198
1380 PRINT:
      PRINT "ENTER EAST CARDS:"
1390 PRINT
1400 FOR I = 14 TO 26
1405 INPUT A$
1410 OK = 0
1420 FOR M = 1 TO 52:
      IF A$#SYM$(2 * M - 1,2 * M) THEN 1460
1440 OK = M:
      M = 52
1460 NEXT M
1480 IF OK > 0 THEN 1500:
      TAB 5:
      PRINT "*** INVALID CARD - REENTER ***":
      CALL -198:
      GOTO 1405
1500 IF CHECK(OK) = 0 THEN 1540
1520 TAB 5:
      PRINT "*** CARD ALREADY USED ***":
      CALL -198:
      GOTO 1405
1540 CHECK(OK) = 1:
      DEAL(I) = OK
1600 NEXT I
1660 CALL -936:
      CALL -198:
      CALL -198
1680 PRINT:
      PRINT "ENTER SOUTH CARDS:"
1690 PRINT
1700 FOR I = 27 TO 39
1705 INPUT A$
```

```
1710 OK = 0
1720 FOR M = 1 TO 52:
     IF A$#SYM$(2 * M - 1,2 * M) THEN 1760
1740 OK = M:
     M = 52
1760 NEXT M
1780 IF OK > 0 THEN 1800:
     TAB 5:
     PRINT "*** INVALID CARD - REENTER ***":
     CALL -198:
     GOTO 1705
1800 IF CHECK(OK) = 0 THEN 1840
1820 TAB 5:
     PRINT "*** CARD ALREADY USED ***":
     CALL -198:
     GOTO 1705
1840 CHECK(OK) = 1:
     DEAL(I) = OK
1900 NEXT I
1960 CALL -936:
     CALL -198:
     CALL -198
1980 PRINT:
     PRINT "ENTER WEST CARDS:"
1990 PRINT
2000 FOR I = 40 TO 52
2005 INPUT A$
2010 OK = 0
2020 FOR M = 1 TO 52:
     IF A$#SYM$(2 * M - 1,2 * M) THEN 2060
2040 OK = M:
     M = 52
2060 NEXT M
2080 IF OK > 0 THEN 2100:
     TAB 5:
     PRINT "*** INVALID CARD - REENTER ***":
     CALL -198:
     GOTO 2005
2100 IF CHECK(OK) = 0 THEN 2140
2120 TAB 5:
     PRINT "*** CARD ALREADY USED ***":
     CALL -198:
     GOTO 2005
2140 CHECK(OK) = 1:
     DEAL(I) = OK
2200 NEXT I
```

```
2300 CALL -936:
     CALL -198:
     CALL -198
2320 PRINT:
     INPUT "WHO DEALT THIS MESS (N/E/S/W) ? ",A$
2340 Q = 4 * (A$="W") + 3 * (A$="S") + 2 * (A$="E") +
(A$="N")
2360 IF Q = 0 THEN 2320
2380 PRINT:
     INPUT "ENTER HAND NUMBER (1-99) ",HN
2400 D$ = "<ctrl-D>":
     REM  CNTRL D IN QUOTES
2420 TEMP = 0:
     FOR I = 1 TO 12:
     FOR J = I + 1 TO 13:
     IF DEAL(I) > DEAL(J) THEN 2460
2440 TEMP = DEAL(I):
     DEAL(I) = DEAL(J):
     DEAL(J) = TEMP
2460 NEXT J,I
2480 TEMP = 0:
     FOR I = 14 TO 25:
     FOR J = I + 1 TO 26:
     IF DEAL(I) > DEAL(J) THEN 2500
2490 TEMP = DEAL(I):
     DEAL(I) = DEAL(J):
     DEAL(J) = TEMP
2500 NEXT J,I
2520 TEMP = 0:
     FOR I = 27 TO 38:
     FOR J = I + 1 TO 39:
     IF DEAL(I) > DEAL(J) THEN 2560
2540 TEMP = DEAL(I):
     DEAL(I) = DEAL(J):
     DEAL(J) = TEMP
2560 NEXT J,I
2580 TEMP = 0:
     FOR I = 40 TO 51:
     FOR J = I + 1 TO 52:
     IF DEAL(I) > DEAL(J) THEN 2620
2600 TEMP = DEAL(I):
     DEAL(I) = DEAL(J):
     DEAL(J) = TEMP
2620 NEXT J,I
2680 PRINT D$;"NOMON I,O,C"
2690 CALL -936
```

```
2700 PRINT D$;"OPEN HAND ";HN
2720 PRINT D$;"WRITE HAND ";HN
2740 FOR I = 1 TO 52:
     PRINT DEAL(I):
     NEXT I:
     PRINT Q
2750 PRINT RND (2)
2760 PRINT D$;"CLOSE HAND ";HN
2800 VTAB 22:
     PRINT "HAND ";HN;" SAVED"
3000 VTAB 23:
     INPUT "BUILD MORE ? (Y/N) ",Z$
3010 IF Z$="Y" THEN 100
3020 IF Z$#"N" THEN 3000
3030 PRINT D$;"RUN TRIK 1.0"
```

Hand File Structures

Each of the HAND files has a total of 54 values stores in it which describe the entire saved hand.

While each file is actually two sectors in the disk or 256 bytes long, the actual data is only $96 bytes or in decimal, 150 bytes.

The file shown below is the contents of HAND1 on the disk:

```
        0  1  2  3  4  5  6  7  8  9  A  B  C  D  E  F
00000 : B5 B1 8D B4 B7 8D B4 B6 8D B4 B4 8D B4 B2 8D B4 : 51M47M46M44M42M4
00010 : B0 8D B3 B6 8D B3 B0 8D B2 B9 8D B2 B8 8D B1 B8 : 0M36M30M29M28M18
00020 : 8D B1 B2 8D B3 8D B4 B8 8D B3 B9 8D B3 B8 8D B3 : M12M3M48M39M38M3
00030 : B7 8D B3 B3 8D B2 B3 8D B2 B2 8D B1 B6 8D B1 B5 : 7M33M23M22M16M15
00040 : 8D B6 8D B5 8D B4 8D B1 8D B5 B2 8D B5 B0 8D B4 : M6M5M4M1M52M50M4
00050 : B9 8D B4 B1 8D B3 B1 8D B2 B6 8D B2 B5 8D B1 B3 : 9M41M31M26M25M13
00060 : 8D B1 B1 8D B9 8D B8 8D B7 8D B2 8D B4 B5 8D B4 : M11M9M8M7M2M45M4
00070 : B3 8D B3 B5 8D B3 B4 8D B3 B2 8D B2 B7 8D B2 B4 : 3M35M34M32M27M24
00080 : 8D B2 B1 8D B2 B0 8D B1 B9 8D B1 B7 8D B1 B4 8D : M21M20M19M17M14M
00090 : B1 B0 8D B4 8D B0 8D 00 00 00 00 00 00 00 00 00 : 10M4M0M.........
000A0 : 00 00 00 00 00 00 00 00 00 00 00 00 00 00 00 00 : ................
000B0 : 00 00 00 00 00 00 00 00 00 00 00 00 00 00 00 00 : ................
000C0 : 00 00 00 00 00 00 00 00 00 00 00 00 00 00 00 00 : ................
000D0 : 00 00 00 00 00 00 00 00 00 00 00 00 00 00 00 00 : ................
000E0 : 00 00 00 00 00 00 00 00 00 00 00 00 00 00 00 00 : ................
000F0 : 00 00 00 00 00 00 00 00 00 00 00 00 00 00 00 00 : ................
```

This structure and length is exactly the same for all of the HAND files and will be the same for HAND files that you create or save from within the game.

www.ingramcontent.com/pod-product-compliance
Lightning Source LLC
Chambersburg PA
CBHW071225170526
45165CB00003B/997